EXPLORE BRITAIN'S
VILLAGES

Produced by AA Publishing

EXPLORE BRITAIN'S
VILLAGES

by Susan Gordon

Copy Editor: Rebecca Snelling

AA Publishing, a trading name of Automobile Association Developments Limited, whose registered office is Norfolk House, Priestley Road, Basingstoke, Hampshire RG24 9NY. Registered number 1878835.

A catalogue record for this book is available from the British Library.

ISBN h/b 0 7495 0684 9
        s/b 0 7495 0774 8

Colour origination by L.C. Repro and Sons Ltd, Aldermaston.
Printed and bound by Graficromo SA, Cordoba, Spain.

The contents of this book are believed correct at the time of printing. Nevertheless, the Publishers cannot accept responsibility for errors or omissions, or for changes in details given.

Acknowledgements: all photographs are held in the Automobile Association's own library with contributions as follows:

F/Cover H. Williams, B/Cover P. Enticknap, Spine R. Strange, 8 S.Gregory, 10/11 P.Baker, 11 T.Woodcock, 12/13 D.Forss, 13 A.Lawson, 14 P.Baker, 15 H.Williams, 16, 17, A.Baker, 18 A.Souter, 20 A.Baker, 21 R.Czaja, 22, 23 A.Baker, 24 T. Teegan, 25, 26 A.Lawson, 27 A.Baker, 28 A.Lawson, 29 A.Lawson, 30 T.Teegan, 31, 32 P.Baker, 33 A.Lawson, 34, 35 A.Baker, 36/7, 37 A.Souter, 38 A.Lawson, 39 T.Teegan, 41 S&O Matthews,43 A.Baker, 44 D.Forss, 46 S&O Matthews, 47 D.Forss, 48, 49 S&O Matthews, 50 D.Forss, 51 D.Noble, 52 S&O Matthews, 53 D.Forss, 54 M.Adelman, 55, 56 S&O Matthews, 57 M. Trelawny, 58 W.Voysey, 59 P.Eden, 60 V.Greaves, 61 D.Forss, 62 M.Birkitt, 63 S&O Matthews, 64, 65 D.Forss, 66, 67 S&O Matthews, 69, 70 D.Forss, 72 M.Adelman, 73 V.Greaves, 74 T.Woodcock, 75 V.Greaves, 76, 77 A.Souter, 78 T.Woodcock, 79 R.Newton, 80 S&O Matthews, 81 A.Tryner, 82 V.Greaves, 83 P.Baker, 84 V.Greaves, 85 S&O Matthews, 86 W.Voysey, 87, 88 S&O Matthews, 89 A.Souter, 90 M.Birkitt, 91 A.Tryner, 92 J.Gravell, 95 A.Baker, 96 R.Newton, 97 A.Baker, 98, 99 J.Gravell, 100, 101 T.Timms, 102 A.Baker, 103 R.Rainford, 104 H.Williams, 105 J.Gravell, 106/7, 107 A.Baker, 108 H.Williams, 109 T.Timms, 110 A.Molyneux, 111 H.Williams, 112 A.Baker, 114 J.Beazley, 115 M.Trelawny, 116 G.Rowatt, 117 E.Bowness, 118 S.Gregory, 119 G.Rowatt, 120 S.Beer, 121 J.Beazley, 123a V.Greaves, 123b R.Eames, 124, 125 E.Bowness, 126, 127 A.Baker, 128 M.Trelawny, 129 R.Eames, 130 A.Baker, 131, 132 R.Newton, 133 J.Beazley, 135 S.King, 136 J.Beazley, 137 D.Forss, 138 J. Carnie, 140 R.Weir, 141 P.Sharp, 142 F.Raffles, 143 J.Beazley, 144 J.Carnie, 145 M.Taylor, 147 P.Sharp, 148/9, 149 D.Hardley, 150 M.Taylor, 151 M.Taylor, 152 R.Weir, 153 J.Beazley, 154 R.Weir, 155, 156 J.Beazley, 158 J.Carnie, 158 J.Beazley.

CONTENTS

Location map
6
Introduction
8

Index
160

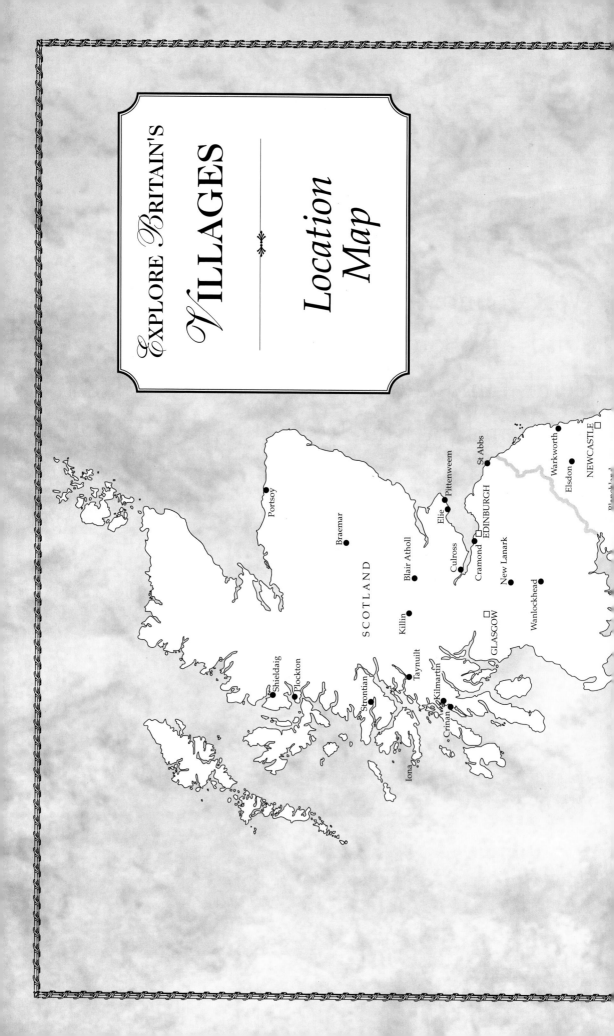

Contemplating the village green at Sinnington, North Yorkshire

INTRODUCTION

Stands the Church clock at ten to three?
And is there honey still for tea?

Rupert Brooke, 'The Old Vicarage, Grantchester'

We all know the poetic vision of village life, the stuff of Christmas calendars: the quaint cottages sitting cosily in traditional gardens; the church with its weekly flower rota and annual fête; Archers mixing with Grundys in classless companionship over a glass of beer in the pub; old George making his way along to the shop for his favourite brand of pickle and the latest gossip; children skipping up the path to school; ducks pottering on the pond or stream; perhaps a game of cricket on the green.

Until about 150 years ago most people in this country lived in villages. Then, lured to the new industrial cities during the years of agricultural depression, people left the countryside in droves; yet, to this day the city dweller has a nostalgia for village life. Tough though it often was, life was

the village: it was home and family, workplace and leisure centre, and it is that all-embracing and self-sufficient community, where life is as whole-some as free range eggs, which is idealised in the chocolate box image.

The casual visitor to a village all too easily sees not only the present coloured by the past, but also the past coloured by the present. There is little now, for instance, that speaks immediately of the squalor and hardship of life in the old days (we see beautiful half-timbering or pretty terraced cottages), of the complete disruption to daily life caused by the dissolution of the monasteries (we see romantic ruins), or of the appalling dispossessions which the parliam-entary enclosures brought for agricultural workers (we see only mature hedgerows and drystone walling). There is nothing to show

The church, the Inn, the Hall between,
The cob-built dwellings round the green,
The village school where once it seems
Summer was constant. Are they dreams
That conjure up those far-gone days
Of village life and village ways?

Extract from the poem 'The Village, A townsman's lament',
by Peter Brereton from his *Touring Guide*
to English Villages

Much of the grey Purbeck stone of which the village of Corfe Castle is built was taken from the castle ruins

how entire villages were wiped out by the plague in the 14th century, and the list of names on the war memorial can only hint at the devastating blow dealt to the village workforce by two world wars. Undoubtedly, the village has to bend to the wind.

Fortune's ebb and flow

Britain had for centuries been covered in hamlets and farmsteads, roads and fields by the time the Saxons, Angles and Jutes arrived in the 5th century AD, and the remains of early settlements can be seen all over the country. Nevertheless, it seems the compact and settled village we know today only came into being with the establishment of the Norman manorial system in the 11th century, when lords of the manor wanted a permanent workforce and serfs realised the benefits of living in a more ordered and settled community.

Since those early times villages have been built and rebuilt over and over again as rivers have silted up and shifted course; forests have been cut down, coppiced and replanted; fields have been enlarged, enclosed and opened up again; roads and motorways have been built and realigned; railways have been constructed and closed. Villages have not always survived the changes, and many fell prey to the all-devouring

As one who long in populous city pent,
Where houses thick and sewers annoy the air,
Forth issuing on a summer's morn to breathe
Among the pleasant villages and farms
Adjoin'd, from each thing met conceives delight.

John Milton (1608–1674), *Paradise Lost*

The forlorn arched doorway of a church which disappeared long since stands beside a farm at Pickford in Leicestershire, deserted in its turn

Black Death, which struck in 1349 at a time when the rural population was already debilitated and in decline. Sometimes, robbed of their livelihood, like the crofters of Scotland in the 19th century, people were forced to desert their villages. And it is easy to forget how helpless our ancestors were in the face of a raging fire that could sweep through their village and destroy every one of their houses of wood and straw in the time it takes us to phone for a fire engine.

The village location

The first thing we observe as we set out to explore Britain's villages, before we get even as far as the sign telling us the name of the place, is the landscape in which the village is set. The environment often dictates not only the siting of the village, but also its lay-out and appearance. In some areas, like the mountains of Wales, the landscape is itself so powerful that the village seems almost insignificant. In the flat landscape of the East Anglian Fens, on the other hand, the view for miles can be dominated by those great cathedral-like parish churches sailing over the fields, village in tow. Little fishing villages in Cornwall cling for their lives to granite cliffs, while the cottages of the Cotswolds seem to have emerged, quietly, from their limestone hills.

Early villages grew up in river valleys, or near a spring, positioned for ready access to fresh water and fertile land, while later villages developed around a water supply for industrial reasons – for the fulling of cloth at Kersey in Suffolk, for instance. Coastal villages are set where safe harbours could be built for fishing, or, like Cley in Norfolk, for trade with France and the Low Countries. Other villages along the south-eastern coasts, such as Winchelsea and Appledore, were developed for purposes of defence. Sometimes a village grew up because there was a plentiful supply of timber in the region, to provide fuel for iron-smelting – although, in the examples of Burwash and Taynuilt, where all

Poynings, in West Sussex, extends along the road and away from the church

the trees are gone, this is no longer apparent. The natural resources of the hills and mountains of Wales, the north of England and Scotland led to the development of mining communities like Dinas Mawddwy, Stanhope and Wanlockhead. Commanding hilltops became the sites for the castles – and the villages they spawned – of Corfe in Dorset, Warkworth in Northumberland and New Radnor in Powys.

Tracing village history

Once over the threshold, and through any recent peripheral housing, the village's original lay-out can usually be traced. Nucleated villages cluster round a green, an old market square or

a church, with streets radiating out, while the linear village spreads along one main artery, a road or a river, with streets running off at right angles. In another easily recognisable type, separate nuclei have developed – one around the church, another around a green, perhaps a third on a modern estate. And then there is the settlement that has grown up without any particular focus or plan, higgledy-piggledy. Most distinctive of all, perhaps, are the 'planned' villages, and one or two examples of a planned, grid lay-out exist from medieval days. In the 18th and 19th centuries 'landlord' villages were either remodelled or built from scratch as part of a new landscaping scheme.

More recently, a few villages have been planned and developed by local authorities. Finally, there is the model village, built by successful industrialists around their factories to house their workers and cater for their every need. Examples of all these types are to be found in this book.

The face first presented by a village is determined by the local building material. Flick through the pages here and you will glimpse granite and cob, limestone and sandstone, flint and millstone grit, half-timbering and harling, and brick that varies in colour from yellow to red to grey to brown. There is slate and thatch, stone slab tile and pantile. Regional diversity of housing material was largely lost after the Industrial Revolution, with easy transport and mass production of brick, and it is only recently that local planners have woken up to the importance of preserving our rich vernacular variety. For decades new village housing has been at best undistinguished and at worst a positive eyesore. Now any new building in a village stands a good chance of being sympathetic in style, and those days are gone when sheds transmogrified into double garages

Thatching is one rural industry which has thrived in recent years, thanks in part to the availability of council grants. This Devon cottage is receiving a new, golden roof of long straw

Well-worn village stocks still stand at Newton Abbas

A church in the fields is suddenly surprised, like a hare peering over a patch of oats

Edmund Blunden, *English Villages* (1941)

and barns into bijou residences without the batting of an eyelid.

The picture a village presents to the outside world is also determined by its gardens and open spaces. The village green is a feature of English villages (there are very few in Scotland or Wales) that is steeped in history and often has changed less than many of the buildings around it. Each green is unique in size and shape, but all would have been used to keep livestock safe at night, and often the animals' watering place, the pond, survives today. It is around this focal point that the village pump, the stocks and lock-up, and the village war memorial are often to be found. It is generally the site, too, of the children's playground and the village football pitch. It may well be where bonfire night celebrations are held.

Old stone and mellow brick are a beautiful foil for the rambling roses, long-established herbaceous borders, old orchards and vegetable patches of the traditional village garden. However, as the village's links with the surrounding fields are lost and it

becomes more and more the preserve of the urban commuter, so, it seems, does the cow parsley at the gate fall victim to the strimmer, while the vegetables in the front garden give way to the neatly mown lawn and the hanging basket that belong to suburbia.

Cornerstones, then and now

The most notable single building in a village is usually its parish church, and it has been estimated that of a total of some 17,000, about 8,000 were built by the Normans, sometimes on the site of an earlier place of worship, indicating great continuity over the

A winding lane leads down the hill to the Gloucestershire village of Bibury

years. Magnificently endowed by lords of the manor anxious to display their wealth and ensure eternity as best they could, and often enlarged by successive generations, the medieval parish church is an incomparable legacy, often apparently out of all proportion to the size of its modern-day congregation. And therein lies a major problem – how to maintain these fine buildings on modern day funding? The village parson nowadays may have four or five churches under his wing, and at any time the parishioners of at least one of these will be desperately trying to raise cash to patch up a roof or repair an

organ. Some churches have been declared redundant, and many Nonconformist chapels have been converted to other uses.

The lord of the manor usually built himself a comfortable home near the church he had endowed, and many of these have survived from Elizabethan days onwards, extended or reconstructed according to dictates of need or fashion. In feudal days the squire had close control of the village, with every aspect of his tenants' lives dependent upon his will and his pocket. In some villages the 'big house' is still lived in by the family, and their influence may still be felt

The ancient inn at Lacock is preserved, like the rest of this Wiltshire village, by the National Trust

The other great time-honoured village institution is the pub. Originally the brewhouse or a coaching inn, it is the place where darts and skittles are played as gossip is exchanged and deals are made – for every village has its own economy, whereby potatoes are swapped for logs, and curtains are made in return for piano lessons. This unique part of our heritage is also struggling for survival – lose it and the community becomes a dormitory.

The village of today

The village is feeling its cornerstones eroded. We complain at the failure to provide adequate public transport for rural areas. We also regret the fact that

in the village. Other manor houses, like parsonages, may have become too costly to run and have been put to some alternative use.

Another bastion of the village is the school. Most date to the Victorian era, some originally being 'dame' schools, and many being founded by the parson. To a village the school is a vital focus of its community, and the environment and education it offers children is one of the things that incomers set great store by. Resources and skills are often shared between neighbouring schools, and yet, with falling rolls, rising maintenance costs and educational reforms, a cloud hangs over the small village school.

Once upon a time every village would have had its own butcher, baker and candlestick-maker. Today, many villages have just one general stores-cum-post office, and even that has for some time now been under threat from the ever-spawning supermarkets, out-of-town retail parks, and the establishment of Sunday trading. The lucky ones may survive on the passing trade of a main road, or the custom generated by summer tourists. Occasionally, an enterprising group of villagers has got together to set up a community shop. If the village does not support its shop, it can easily find itself not only without a lifeline for those who have no private transport, but also without a social focus.

What memories hang about this gaunt old room, with its tall windows, its faint green walls and iron girders from which, high up in the roof, glare down the unshaded electric bulbs!... all our lives through, from schooldays among the desks and blackboards to the time when, as pensioners, we come here for the Old Friends annual party, the school has been the centre of our social existence.

WI scrapbook from Smarden, Kent, quoted by Paul Jennings in *The Living Village* (1968)

those who have lived and worked in the village all their lives are outnumbered by newcomers who commute (by car) to work in the towns. Yet, ironically, it is often just this new blood that is articulate and energetic enough to initiate the running of community buses, the setting up of care groups, the rebuilding of community halls, the fight to keep the school, the campaign for low-cost housing for senior citizens and young people pushed out by privatisation of council housing and escalating house prices. And, although their emigration to the village fuels the inflation of property values, it is they who revive the older, run-down properties. Determined they are that the village will survive as a modern-dress version of that all-caring, self-sufficient idyll of our nostalgic dreams. Tourism is an important, expanding village industry, and in some areas small businesses are helping breathe new life into the community.

The village of today is facing change, but only as the next stage in a continuous process of evolution. In the following pages the reader is taken on an exploration of over 100 villages. The stories they have to tell are infinitely varied, but one thing is certain: the hands of the church clock may stand for ever at ten to three, but for the people living in its shadow time has never stood still.

The pretty Yorkshire village of Kettlewell thrives on the passing trade of tourists and walkers, out to explore the Dales

An old Cotswold outer stairway

WEST COUNTRY

Most of the cottages were built of Cotswold stone and were roofed by split-stone tiles. The tiles grew a kind of golden moss which sparkled like crystallised honey. Behind the cottages were long steep gardens full of cabbages, fruit-bushes, rabbit-hutches, earth-closets, bicycles and pigeon-lofts...

Laurie Lee,
Cider with Rosie

AVEBURY
Wiltshire

In 1663 the diarist John Aubrey wrote that the prehistoric site of Avebury 'does as much exceed Stonehenge in greatness as a cathedral does a parish church'. The 28 acre (11.3ha) complex is indeed very much larger and arguably more impressive than that of its more famous and now, sadly, somewhat tawdry sister. It also predates Stonehenge, making it the place, according to Sir John Betjeman, where the story of English architecture begins.

Sarsen stones at the door of the Red Lion

To enter this unique village and observe its daily life, apparently unaffected by the immense Neolithic stone circle within which it partly stands, is to feel the centuries concertina into timelessness. The circle, with its gaunt stones and its vast bank and ditch, was probably in use as a major ceremonial centre from c.2500BC. In the early Middle Ages, however, with the arrival of the first Christian chapel at Avebury, villagers set about burying some of the pagan stones. By the 18th century, when the village was expanding, other stones were broken up and these squarish blocks of sarsen can be seen in several of the buildings, including the old school, Silbury House and the Methodist chapel. As recently as the early 1960s the National Trust seriously considered demolishing parts of the village within the circle, including the manorial aisled barn that now houses the Museum of Wiltshire Folk Life. The uneasy partnership between village and prehistoric site seems now to have settled into mutual forbearance, with the thatched pub plying its trade in the shadow of the stones. The church, of Saxon and Norman origins, is remarkable for its south doorway, font and rood screen, and sits prettily with the Elizabethan manor house just outside the earthwork. Other attractive houses within and without the circle are built of brick, flint or cob, some timber-framed, several thatched.

Roses round the door of one of the thatched cottages

BURTON BRADSTOCK
Dorset

3 MILES (5 KM) SOUTH-EAST OF BRIDPORT

The Dorset historian Hutchins made the perhaps doubtful claim that in 1757 a mermaid was washed up on the beach here. However, the charm of the village that lies just inland from the western end of Chesil Beach is something that remains beyond question. Narrow lanes wiggle and wind away from the main road, all packed with pretty houses, their roofs neatly thatched or tiled in local Purbeck stone-slate. The walls of rubble limestone, some colour-washed, are often clad in roses, clematis or ivy. Many of the houses are 17th-century, including the White House by the triangular green, while the Perpendicular church with its central tower dates entirely to the 15th century, except for the surprising and idiosyncratic south aisle designed by E S Prior at the end of the 19th century. The little River Bride works its way through the village to pass though a gap in the cliffs about a mile south. The hills behind the village, some of which have prehistoric hillforts on top, all offer good views over the English Channel. Mermaids or no, smuggling was rife along this stretch of coast in the 18th century and the county's most notorious smuggler, Isaac Gulliver, used the Drove Inn as his contraband distribution centre.

Old weavers' cottages beside the By Brook

CASTLE COMBE
Wiltshire

6 MILES (9.5 KM) NORTH-WEST OF CHIPPENHAM

The Blanket Brothers
The story goes that two Castle Combe brothers by the name of Blanket, finding their weavers' cottage alongside Pack Bridge somewhat chilly, wove a heavy, raised nap cloth which they wrapped around themselves at night for warmth. Others followed suit, naming their new bedcloth after the brothers.

An especially pretty village set in a hollow on the southern edge of the Cotswolds, Castle Combe owes its name to the fortification built here, first by the Romans, then by the Saxons and finally by Walter de Dunstanville, a Norman. Little remains of his castle but he has a splendid tomb in the church, which is itself a fine example of Gothic architecture, built largely on the wealth of the local clothiers. Near by is their 15th-century market cross, its hipped stone roof supported by four heavy posts. The honeyed-stone weavers' cottages, with typical steep, gabled roofs of Cotswold stone tiles, run down the hill to the By Brook. The bigger houses include the old manor house, now a hotel. The old court house may be distinguished by its overhung, half-timbered upper storey. Behind is the old gaol, a wattle-and-daub building now doing time as a shed. There is a stone dovecote and, beyond, the triple-arched packhorse bridge over the By Brook. Castle Combe is popular with visitors, but thankfully their cars are banished to the outskirts and this intimate and well-kept Cotswold village manages to retain its charm and tranquillity.

CHEW MAGNA
Somerset

6 MILES (9.5 KM) SOUTH OF BRISTOL

'*I*t is a praty clothing town, and hath a faire church,' wrote John Leland, reporting on Chew Magna to Henry VIII in 1545. It is still a pretty village today, but any air of prosperity probably has more to do with proximity to Bristol than the cloth trade. The church, partly Norman, is, as so often, the strongest link with the wool era. It is memorable chiefly for the 15th-century tower and its fearsome gang of gargoyles. Inside is a large rood screen, and a wooden tomb effigy over which an air of mystery hangs. It claims to be Sir John de Hauteville, and he lies, rather uncomfortably, on his side, propped up on one elbow, legs crossed, one foot resting on an upright lion. He wears 14th-century armour, but other details do not tie up with that date. Near the church is a striking 16th-century building known either as the Old Schoolroom (for that is what it was from 1842 to 1894) or the Church Alehouse, one-time venue for parish parties. Chew Court, once part of the Bishop of Bath and Wells's Palace of Chew, has an imposing gateway above which is the old courtroom. The High Street is flanked by unusual raised pavements, some good Georgian houses and pleasant cottages.

Tun Bridge
A buttress on the eastern side of the bridge holds a stone trough 'well'. When smallpox was rife in the village this was filled with disinfectant and farmers, bringing their goods for sale only as far as the bridge, would collect their money from the well.

The shaft of an old preaching cross in the churchyard

*The pump at the southern
end of Fore Street, installed
for the use of farmers at
the market*

CHULMLEIGH
Devon

15 MILES (24 KM) SOUTH-EAST OF BARNSTAPLE

The Barnstaple Inn, a thatched, granite building on the northern fringes, is dated 1633 but may be of earlier origin. At that time it was a local court-house and had a gibbet over the door for the immediate execution of convicted offenders.

Chulmleigh is a good example of how changing transportation systems can affect fortune's ebb and flow. The village grew up at the junction of five ancient roads and developed as an important market centre in what was, even before Domesday, a prosperous sheep-farming area. Its 15th-century church is a proud reminder of those days, its granite tower visible for miles around. Inside is an excellent, wide rood screen and a wagon roof with good bosses and ribs supported by the outspread wings of 38 carved angels. The market was held in Fore Street, where its old pump still stands. The King's Arms, with its grand façade, was a busy coaching inn with extensive stabling

for the horses. In 1830, however, a new turnpike from Exeter to Barnstaple bypassed the town (meaning loss of trade for the King's Arms of course) and in 1854 the railway came and markets moved to stations. Even before then, competition from the North had dealt a blow to the woollen trade, and soon improvements in farming practices led to further unemployment. Add to this two disastrous fires in the 19th century, and Chulmleigh's days of prosperity were numbered. Some wonderful old merchants' houses, many cob, stone and thatched cottages, as well as a medieval toll-house, have survived, however, and Chulmleigh today is a fascinating place to explore.

CLOVELLY
Devon

Clovelly is one of England's show-places, and has been since Kingsley and Dickens drew attention to it in the 19th century. That it remains both well-preserved and remarkably unspoilt is due largely to the lords of the manor, the Hamlyns. In particular, Christine Hamlyn, whose initials can be seen on many of the houses, kept the motor car away and to this day all vehicles have to be left at the top of the village. Sledges are used to carry provisions down the one very steep, cobbled street that leads down 400ft (122m) to the pretty harbour, built when fishing first became profitable in the 16th century.

So steep and narrow is the High Street (called Up-along or Down-along, according to which way you are going) that the little whitewashed houses spill down on both sides in a great jumble, one on top of the other. Its setting in a thickly wooded cleft is best appreciated from the pier. These woods, as well as the 3-mile (4.8km) Hobby Drive, were planted by an early 19th-century Hamlyn. In the church, half a mile above and away from the village, are monuments to earlier lords of the manor, the Careys, as well as Hamlyns, and one to Charles Kingsley, whose *Westward Ho!* and *The Water Babies* were written here.

Three fishers went sailing away to the west,
Away to the west as the sun went down;
Each thought on the woman who loved him the best,
And the children stood watching them out of the town.

Charles Kingsley, 'The Three Fishers'

Up-along…or Down-along

COCKINGTON
Devon

1 ½ MILES (2.5 KM) WEST OF TORQUAY

*I*t is not often one can say that a village's recent history may be as significant as its past. During World War II the Prudential Building Society evacuated its staff to Torquay, and a rapport built up with the locals so that, when the privately owned Cockington Estate was about to be split up, the Prudential decided to invest in its thatched cottages and shops en bloc, maintaining them in traditional style and thus preserving on the outskirts of Torquay this quaint Domesday village. Some of the cottages have Saxon origins and the 13th- and 14th-century red sandstone church has Norman foundations. The old forge dates from the 14th century. The only modern building is the thatched Drum Inn,

built harmoniously by Sir Edwin Lutyens in 1934. Cockington Court, the Elizabethan manor of the Carys and then of the Mallocks who added its façade, is owned by Torbay Borough Council and is now home to the Devon Rural Skills Trust, who provide workspace for such threatened craftsworkers as the blacksmith, hurdlemaker and thatcher. Its grounds are a designated country park, open to all. For decades now horse-drawn carriages have brought visitors out here from Torquay seafront. These visitors have inevitably brought with them such accoutrements of tourism as litter bins and public conveniences, but the village's immediate environment is assured development in a natural and harmonious way.

Horse-drawn carriages bring visitors to this 'olde-worlde' village and its country park

Village corner, Duntisbourne Abbots

DUNTISBOURNE ABBOTS
Gloucestershire

6 MILES (9.5 KM) NORTH-WEST OF CIRENCESTER

Duntisbourne Abbots is the most northerly of a group of four Duntisbournes. As picturesque as many another Cotswold village, they also have strong associations with the followers of William Morris, who first popularised the Cotswolds. In the parish of Duntisbourne Rouse, to the south-west of the village, lies Pinbury Park, where Ernest Gimson, brilliant interpreter of the Arts and Crafts movement, and his fellow designer-craftsmen, the Barnsley brothers, came to live at the beginning of the century. Cotswold Farm, near Duntisbourne Abbots, was enlarged by Sidney Barnsley in 1926 and has a window by Edward Burne-Jones. In medieval times Duntisbourne Abbots, as indicated by its name, belonged to the Abbot of Gloucester. His mainly Norman but much restored church is approached through a lych-gate, past some good table tombs. Better known is the small church at Duntisbourne Rouse, which has Saxon origins. Making use of the slope on which it stands, the Normans built a crypt under the chancel. The little tower has a saddleback roof and the medieval misericords are to be relished. Duntisbourne Leer, one of several places in the valley where the River Churn has to be forded, and Middle Duntisbourne complete this beautifully situated quartet of mellow Cotswold villages.

FRAMPTON ON SEVERN
Gloucestershire

8 MILES (13 KM) SOUTH OF GLOUCESTER

*O*ne of the prerequisites of a perfect village is a green, but few can rival Frampton's. Its 22 acres (9ha), divided by the road that runs through the village, make it one of England's largest, and three ponds and a cricket pitch lie within it. Known as Rosamund's Green, it lends added dignity to the half-timbered and Georgian houses that line its sides. Henry II's mistress, 'Fair Rosamund', Jane Clifford, is said to have been born here. Kept by Henry in a house in Woodstock surrounded by a maze, she is reputed to have been poisoned by Henry's Queen Eleanor, who found her way through the maze by following a thread of the king's cloak.

The seat of the Clifford family is Frampton Court, the most imposing house on the green, though partly hidden by trees. Built in the 1730s in Vanbrugh style, probably by John Strachan of Bristol, it has low wings on either side and handsome chimneys. In the 1980s a beautiful collection of Victorian flower paintings, done by lady members of the family, was discovered in an attic and published as *The Frampton Flora*. Visible from the road is William Halfpenny's 'Strawberry Hill' Gothic orangery, with pretty ogee windows. In front of it, but not visible from the green, is a rectangular canal. On the other side of the green is the family's 15th-century,

Manor Farm

partly half-timbered manor house. Further down the green the houses are smaller and less spaced out, but none the less attractive, some gabled and thatched. Eventually the road bends away from the green to wind through the rest of the village, finally reaching the church, which is set apart from the village beside the Sharpness Canal. The canal-keeper's Doric-style house is not far away and boats pass within yards of the church. It dates mainly from the 14th century, with some 15th-century additions, and with most of its windows being of clear glass it is pleasantly light and airy. There is some medieval glass and the lead font is one of six similar ones surviving in Gloucestershire dated to around 1250–75. There are some notable monuments, particularly the tablet made by John Pearce, 'statuary and diagraphist', in memory of his brothers.

A Georgian house on Rosamund's Green

*New housing in a
sympathetic style*

LUCCOMBE
Somerset

4 MILES (6.5 KM) SOUTH-EAST OF PORLOCK

During the Civil War,
Parliamentarians tried to arrest
Luccombe's Royalist vicar,
Henry Byam. He escaped,
however, to join Charles I. At
the Restoration, Byam was
returned as Vicar of Luccombe,
Canon of Exeter and
Prebendary of Wales, to much
local rejoicing.

*L*uccombe is one of the prettiest villages on the Holnicote Estate, an area of Exmoor beneath Dunkery Beacon that is owned by the National Trust. Steep, narrow lanes lead to the village through fields of red earth bounded by red sandstone walls. It is the cottages that make Luccombe attractive. Most are of cob, cream-washed with a black skirting at the base, and have uneven thatched roofs with overhanging eaves. Until it was given to the National Trust in 1944, the Holnicote Estate was owned by the Acland family. In the early 19th century the 10th Baronet Acland did much to improve the estate and many of the 16th- and 17th-century cottages were extended by raising the roofs, making attic rooms with dormer windows. Rounded bread ovens, projecting from one corner, can still be seen on some cottages. In recent years a few new houses have been built in sympathetic style by a local housing association, to provide accommodation in an area where few local people can afford it any more. The church is a good one – high and light, with a wagon roof decorated with large bosses and some glass in Arts and Crafts style. It is depicted in Samuel Palmer's famous painting, 'Coming out of Evening Church'.

MILTON ABBAS
Dorset

*I*n the 1770s Joseph Damer, later Earl of Dorchester, had a mansion built for himself next to the abbey church on the site of the ancient monastery that gave Milton Abbas its name. He liked his mansion (designed by Sir William Chambers and Sir James Wyatt), but he didn't like the view which was spoilt by the market town that had grown up around the abbey. So he had it all demolished (except for one thatched cottage which nicely added a touch of rustic charm to 'Capability' Brown's landscaping plans). He did re-house some of the folk dislodged from the eyesore, however, and thus came about this early, consciously picturesque example of a planned or 'model' village. A mile from the big house, which is now a public school, and tucked away in a wooded valley, is the single street of 20 identical pairs of thatched, cob cottages, all of which were washed yellow at the time of completion. Damer had the old almshouses removed here from the original village – a good PR touch, perhaps, but it also provided some of the old-world charm that he was after. The church was built in the mid-1780s. The open lawns in front of the cottages create the effect of a village green, and there is a thatched pub at one end and, at the other, the lake that Damer had made.

The village still looks much the same as when Lord Dorchester created it

MONTACUTE
Somerset

4 MILES (6.5 KM) WEST OF YEOVIL

Mons Acutus

The original *mons acutus*, above the village, is St Michael's Hill. A miracle-working cross that was said to have cured King Harold of paralysis was found here in the 11th century. The folly on top of the hill was built by the Phelips family in 1760.

The drinking fountain in the centre of the village

A close look at the ground plan and street names of the village of Montacute will reveal its unusual origins as two boroughs. William the Conqueror's half-brother, Robert de Mortain, established Bishopston (the name of the street that runs north from the church) in about 1100, but was forced to give it to the Abbey of Cluny in France which founded a priory here in 1102. The village flourished as a woollen centre under the priory until it was dissolved and sold by Henry VIII in 1539. Today only its gatehouse and names such as Abbey Farm, Priory Pond and Priory Field remind us of its existence. The Borough, the spacious main square, marks the centre of the second borough, added alongside in 1240. The beautifully golden-coloured 17th- and 18th-century houses are built of stone from nearby Ham Hill, with stone-mullioned windows and mellow, reddish-tiled roofs. Terraced cottages in South Street were weavers' homes when trade flourished here again in the 18th century. The church has a Norman chancel arch and a fine Somerset tower. But the jewel in Montacute's crown is Montacute House. Delicate, dignified, warm and welcoming, it is one of the country's dearest Elizabethan houses. It was built between about 1590 and 1600 for lawyer Edward Phelips, whose family lived here for 300 years, and is now in the care of the National Trust.

Stargazy Pie
This is a local dish made with whole fish whose heads stick out through the pastry crust. Traditionally, it is eaten here on Tom Bawcock's Eve, 23 December. Tom was a Mousehole fisherman who is said to have saved the villagers from starvation after going out in a storm and bringing back a huge catch of seven different kinds of fish.

Houses cluster round the granite harbour

MOUSEHOLE
Cornwall

2 MILES (3 KM) SOUTH OF PENZANCE

Phoenician tin merchants came here 2,500 years ago and it is thought the name Mousehole (pronounced 'Mowzel') may derive from their word for watering place. A little more recently, in 1595, the village fell victim to 200 Spaniards who landed here from four galleons, raping the women and burning just about all the houses bar the former manor house in Keigwin Street. Since then the village has rebuilt itself in the narrow streets and alleys that twist uphill from the curving granite quays of the harbour. This was once the centre of Cornwall's pilchard-fishing industry, but the pilchards had left the Cornish waters by the end of the 19th century and now only a few boats operate from here. Among the grey-brown granite houses, with their lichen-covered slate roofs and splashes of fuschia and hydrangea, stand two large Methodist chapels, a reminder of John Wesley's activities in this area. The village church is some way up the hill, in the parish of Paul. Here may be found a memorial to Dolly Pentreath who died in 1777, allegedly the last person to speak – and swear – solely in Cornish. In 1981 disaster struck the village again when the Penlee lifeboat went down with its entire crew – all Mousehole men.

Cottages line the Nunney Brook

NUNNEY
Somerset

3 MILES (4.8 KM) SOUTH-WEST OF FROME

The Village of Nunney

...perfection, having everything which the heart could desire to make it both lovely and interesting...
Maxwell Fraser

It is not often a village can add a moated medieval castle to a list of ingredients that already satisfies every requirement of a fairy-tale village. But Nunney is exceptional. It is set in a wooded valley at the eastern end of the Mendip Hills; a stream flows past the grey-stone, red-tiled houses and thatched cottages; there is a church on the hill, a fine manor house and a pub. It even has a thatched bus shelter.

The castle dates to 1373, when Sir John De la Mare, recently returned from the war in France with much booty, was given a licence to fortify and crenellate his manse. He placed four mighty, round towers at the corners of a rectangular central block four storeys high. Sir Nikolaus Pevsner says it is of a type found in the north of England; others say it was modelled

on the Bastille in France. During the Civil Wars it was a Royalist stronghold and was eventually beaten into submission by Parliamentarian cannon. Today the romantic ruin, in the care of English Heritage, is reached from the main street by a foot-bridge over what is said to be the deepest water-filled moat in the country. Across the stream and the street from the castle is the church, originally 13th-century but much rebuilt in the 19th century. It has a round Norman font, bits of a Saxon cross and a wall-painting of St George. There are effigies of Sir John (probably) and of subsequent owners of the castle, the Poulets and the Praters. One of the Roundhead cannonballs that wrecked the castle is on display. The Nunney Brook flows down the length of the village and it was this that first brought the village prosperity, when the wool trade was centred on nearby Frome in the late 17th and early 18th centuries. Many of the weavers' cottages in Horn Street carry dates within this period and most of the bigger houses were also built at this time, including Palladian-style Manor Farm. Wool was washed on the sloping cobbled pavement in front of the church, where the medieval market cross stands. The industry declined locally towards the end of the 18th century when mills in the North took all the trade, but at about that time Fussell's ironworks grew up, using the Nunney Brook for power and providing employment well into the 19th century.

The ruined castle and its moat

THE SLAUGHTERS
Gloucestershire

10 MILES (16 KM) WEST OF CHIPPING NORTON

*I*n the heart of the lush Cotswold countryside, the two villages of Lower and Upper Slaughter make a pretty pair. If they are much photographed it is not without justification, for they have a character and charm that belies their gruesome-sounding name. In fact, 'slaughter' is derived from a word meaning no more than 'marshy place'. The River Eye runs through both villages, flowing under picturesque stone footbridges and alongside typically mellow, honey-coloured cottages and houses. In both, the buildings are of the local oolitic limestone, many dating back to the great period of stone building from the mid-16th to the mid-17th century. Most of the roofs are stone-tiled, with gables or dormers, and many of the windows are stone-mullioned, in true Cotswold style.

In Lower Slaughter the red-brick chimney of an early 19th-century corn mill stands out in contrast to the stone-tiled roofs, its waterwheel still intact. The main street runs alongside the river, trees shading the grassy bank

Lower Slaughter, where the River Eye flows broad and shallow

opposite the picture postcard row of houses. Near the church is the former manor house, built in the 17th century for the Whitmore family who continued to be active here until the 1960s. Its dovecote, 16th-century and built like a Cotswold cottage, is one of the largest in the county. But there are lovely houses at every turn. The church has medieval origins but was reconstructed in the 1860s for Charles Shapland Whitmore by Benjamin Ferry. The spire is notable for its fibreglass tip, put into position by a helicopter in the 1960s.

A mile away upstream, the village of Upper Slaughter stands on a grassy hill overlooking the Slaughter Brook, and in among its cluster of cottages and houses are the remains of a Norman motte-and-bailey castle that once dominated the village. Several Norman features survived

19th-century restoration work in the church. Other items of interest here include brasses to the De Slaughter family, who owned the old manor house in the 16th century, and the canopied mortuary chapel of the Reverend F E Witts (d.1854), author of *The Diary of a Cotswold Parson*. His son and grandson succeeded him in the parsonage, now the Lords of the Manor Hotel, and most of the memorials are to the Witts family. Many features of the village remain as they are described in the diary. The group of cottages in the open square, near the churchyard, was remodelled in 1906 by Sir Edwin Lutyens, but since then there has been virtually no new building and the village remains completely in traditional style.

Upper Slaughter: splashes of colour sing out against the mellowed Cotswold stone

The opulent gatehouse to Stanway House

STANTON AND STANWAY
Gloucestershire

3 MILES (5 KM) SOUTH-WEST OF BROADWAY

The Crusoe Connection
Stanway House was the home of Thomas Dover, a privateer, who in 1709 rescued from a desert island the man who inspired Daniel Defoe's *Robinson Crusoe*. Alexander Selkirk had asked to be put ashore on the uninhabited island of Juan Fernandez in 1704, after a row with his ship's captain, and was never taken back on board.

There are many villages, particularly in the Cotswolds, where one landlord has owned the entire village, and the way these villages look now, when many of the houses have been sold off, often still reflects the manner in which the squire managed his or her property. Stanton is one such village, nestling peacefully under woods on the edge of the Cotswold escarpment, as near perfect as can be – yet without the trappings of tourism. The steeply gabled cottages were built in the local golden stone around 1600, but the unity of their appearance today owes much to the restoration work carried out by the village's owner from 1906 to 1937, the architect Philip Stott. The church is Norman and interesting for the 1920s rood screen, organ loft and windows by Sir Ninian Comper. Look out for his wild strawberry signature in the windows.

Stanway has been described as Stanton's aristocratic neighbour. It is a hamlet that consists of little more than the accoutrements of its Jacobean manor house, but each of these is something special. There is a thatched cricket pavilion – set high on staddle stones – by James Barrie, a 14th-century tithe barn, and a war memorial with a fine bronze of St George and lettering by Eric Gill. Most arresting of all, however, is the three-storey, gabled gatehouse. Open to the public at limited times during the summer months, Stanway House itself has the refreshing air of a lived-in home, with family bits and pieces left out on view.

TINTAGEL
Cornwall

5 MILES (8 KM) NORTH-WEST OF CAMELFORD

Geoffrey of Monmouth, in about 1150, put about the story that a fortress here had been the birthplace of King Arthur in the 6th century. The legend has flourished ever since and became especially popular in the Romantic era of the 19th century, when visitors started to flock here. Now, in summer, the place is a tourist honeypot, but come out of season and the magic cannot fail to work. Tintagel village, originally called Trevena, was one of several villages in the parish of Tintagel that grew up, like others, round its manor house. This rare 14th-century building, known as the Old Post Office, is sturdily built with tiny windows in its dark stone walls and a heavy slate roof. But everything else in the village is insubstantial; what is important is 'the island', a precipitous promontory joined to the cliffs by a narrow neck of land. It is an impressive site, lonely and windswept, the waters of the Atlantic swirling relentlessly far below. There are the remains of what some consider to be 6th-century monastic cells, others a tin-trading settlement, but more prominent are the black ruins of a castle built from the 12th century on by Norman earls of Cornwall to keep a watch on the Celts. All too easily the romance of the place takes over and they become the ruins of Arthur's castle.

*On one side lay the Ocean, and on one
Lay a great water, and the moon was full.*

Tennyson, *The Passing of Arthur*

The 14th-century manor house, restored to its 19th-century use as a post office and in the care of the National Trust

Best seen from the river, the 17th-century manor house and its barn make an attractive grouping with the partly Norman, cob-and-flint church

---
❁

TOLPUDDLE
Dorset

7 MILES (11 KM) NORTH-EAST OF DORCHESTER
❁
---

*T*he injustices of village society in days gone by can easily be forgotten, so taken are we with the charm and, so often, the apparent prosperity of Britain's villages today. The story of the Tolpuddle Martyrs, however, permeates every corner of this village, making it the best known of several along the valley of the River Piddle or, as Victorian prudes preferred, Puddle.

In 1833, the year in which slavery was abolished in the British colonies, Dorset farmworkers were being given a weekly wage of seven shillings, three shillings less than the minimum agricultural wage in the south of England. The squirearchy was omnipotent. When George Loveless, a Tolpuddle farm labourer and Methodist lay-preacher, attempted to get a higher wage for his fellow workers he was blocked by local squire and Justice of the Peace, James Frampton. The efforts of the Reverend Warren also came to nothing, so Loveless appealed to the trade union movement. The Grand Lodge of

a Whig and friend of Lord Melbourne, sentenced the men to seven years' transportation to Australia.

George Loveless and his brother James, James Brine, Thomas Stanfield and his son John, and James Hammett, immediately became popular heroes and a nationwide campaign was launched to secure their release. In 1836 the men were granted the king's pardon and returned to this country. Five of them, however, then emigrated to Canada and only James Hammett came back to Tolpuddle, dying a blind man in the workhouse.

Near the centre of the village, on the sloping triangular green, stands an aged sycamore tree under which the martyrs held some of their meetings. Near by, a thatched shelter commemorates the men, as does the gateway to the Methodist chapel. Thomas Standfield's cottage, where their oaths were taken, may be found in the main street, while the whole story is documented in the museum housed in one of the six cottages built in the village in 1933 by the Trades Union Council.

The martyrs' tree, an aged sycamore propped up on posts

Tolpuddle of the Agricultural Labourers' Friendly Society was formed and members swore their oaths of allegiance. Squire Frampton, along with other local landlords, became concerned as membership of the union grew and appealed to the Lord Lieutenant of Dorset, who in turn took the matter to the Whig Home Secretary, Lord Melbourne. Alarmed at these signs of working-class discontent, he pointed out that a law about secret oath-taking that had inadvertently been left on the statute book could be invoked against the union members. As a result six Tolpuddle men were arrested, ostensibly for administering unlawful oaths but in fact for conspiring in an attempt to improve their starvation-level wages. The magistrates, all landowners themselves, sent them for trial at Dorchester Assizes. The judge,

WORTH MATRAVERS
Dorset

3 MILES (5 KM) WEST OF SWANAGE

In the churchyard is the grave of one Benjamin Jesty, who is said to have used his wife and sons as guinea-pigs, inoculating them with cowpox against smallpox. This was in 1774, some 24 years before Sir Edward Jenner published the findings of his similar experiments.

Sunshine lifts the otherwise somewhat austere stone of the houses

The Isle of Purbeck is pitted with old quarries, quarries that produced Purbeck marble, a limestone that polishes like marble and was used in many medieval churches and cathedrals. All the houses of Worth Matravers, built of this greyish stone, were once the homes of local quarrymen and stonemasons. A little uphill from the duck pond is The Square and Compass Inn, which takes its name from the tools of the stonemason's craft, and many of the garden walls display an ammonite or two, revealed during quarrying. Dry-stone walls criss-cross the somewhat treeless landscape that surrounds the compact little village. A short walk down the narrow valley at the head of which it stands (with good views of extensive strip lynchets on either side) leads to clifftop Winspit Quarry, now disused. Stone from here was lowered directly on to sea barges and taken round to Swanage for transport on to London. Swanage was originally just a hamlet in the parish of Worth Matravers, the two churches being connected by a path, now known as The Priest's Way. Worth Matravers Church is especially fine. It needed restoration work in the 19th century, but its tympanum, depicting the Coronation of the Virgin, its beautiful, ornate chancel arch and some windows all date from Norman times.

The granite village that seems to grow out of the landscape

ZENNOR
Cornwall

4 MILES (6 KM) SOUTH-WEST OF ST IVES

West Penwith is Celtic Cornwall at its most inspiring, a patch of England on which modern man has left little mark. The weathered, grey buildings of the village of Zennor huddle together in a dip in this ancient granite landscape, lumps of stone strewn around, trees struggling to beat the gales. The church is old but much altered and is chiefly known for the 15th-century bench-end, now part of a chair, on which is carved the famous mermaid of Zennor who, according to legend, lured the squire's son down to her home beneath the waves. The Wayside Museum depicts the industrial past of the area, also reflected in the name of the pub, the Tinners' Arms, where D H Lawrence drank while living near by during World War I, at work on his novel *Women in Love*. To the north-west of the village are the jagged cliffs of Zennor Head and the rugged stretch of coastline on either side. Just inland, up on the bleak, treeless moorland, is Zennor Quoit, a Neolithic chambered tomb with a capstone 18ft (5.5m) long that was supported on five upright stones until vandalised by farmers in the 19th century. One end now rests on the ground. All around, in the bracken and gorse, are field boundary walls that were built by Iron Age Celtic farmers and have stood, timeless, through the centuries.

A tiny granite village nestling under high shaggy moor-hills, and a big sweep of lovely sea beyond, such a lovely sea, lovelier ever than the Mediterranean…It is all gorse now, flickering with flowers; and then it will be the heather; and then, hundreds of fox gloves. It is the best place I have been in, I think.'
D H Lawrence, writing to J M Murry and Katherine Mansfield from Zennor, March 1916

Ornamental name-plate, Winchelsea

SOUTH AND SOUTH-EAST

———— ✦ ————

No tender-hearted garden crowns,
No bosomed woods adorn
Our blunt, bow-headed, whale-backed Downs
But gnarled and writhen thorn –
Bare slopes where chasing shadows skim,
And through the gaps revealed,
Belt upon belt, the wooded, dim,
Blue goodness of the Weald.

Rudyard Kipling,
'Sussex'

The west tower of the church, a survival from the 13th century

APPLEDORE
Kent

10 MILES (16 KM) SOUTH OF ASHFORD

This peaceful and attractive village on the edge of Romney Marsh started life as a port on the estuary of the River Rother, but in the 13th century violent storms changed the course of the Rother and gradual silting-up left Appledore (meaning 'apple tree') 8 miles (13km) or so inland. Not far enough, however, to escape a raid by the French in 1380 during which they burned the 13th-century church. Its chunky tower survived and the rest was reconstructed shortly afterwards, a little untidily, making plentiful use of timber inside. In 1381 Wat Tyler attacked Horne's Place, a 14th-century farmhouse with a gem of a private chapel. More peaceful days followed, with markets and a fair that had been licensed by Edward III being held in its broad main street. In 1804 there was the threat of another French invasion, under Napoleon, and the Royal Military Canal was built, curving round the marsh. Regular dog-legs meant the whole stretch could be covered by cannon fire. The canal's potential was not forgotten in World War II, when pillboxes were built along its length. Today, Appledore lies quietly to the north of the canal, most of it along the one main street, its buildings a pleasing mix of styles and ages from the 16th century onwards.

AYLESFORD
Kent

3 MILES (5 KM) NORTH-WEST OF MAIDSTONE

There is a record of a bridge spanning the Medway at Aylesford in 1287. In the 14th century this was replaced by the Kentish flagstone bridge that has survived to this day. The view from this bridge is one of the best there is of the picturesque brick-and-half-timbered, steeply gabled cottages. The river once powered the paper mill that has operated here since the turn of the century. Prehistory courses through the veins of this, one of Kent's oldest villages. On the outskirts is Kit's Coty House, the awe-inspiring remains of a Neolithic burial chamber. In AD455 the Britons were defeated in battle here by Jutish invaders, and in 893 the Danes were seen off by King Alfred, while in 918 Edmund Ironside routed Canute and the Vikings. Later, in more peaceful mode, the Carmelites came to England and founded their first friary in this country in Aylesford, in 1240. For 300 years it flourished, until it was given, at the dissolution, to Ann Boleyn's lover, Sir Thomas Wyatt of nearby Allington. The estate stayed in private hands until 1949 when the dispossessed order of Carmelites returned to their home (the first to do so), finding many of the buildings still standing although in need of repair. Fully restored, The Friars' 14th-century cloister, 15th-century Pilgrims' Hall and pottery are open to the public.

THE FLOWER OF CARMEL ONCE CUT DOWN NOW FLOURISHES MORE LUXURIANTLY THAN EVER. (Inscription over the entrance to the main courtyard of The Friars)

On the banks of the Medway, a little-known but attractive waterway

BURPHAM
West Sussex

3 MILES (5 KM) NORTH-EAST OF ARUNDEL

*T*his is a lovely place, at the end of a lane that winds north from the A27, leads round the village, then goes no further. The Saxons built defensive earthworks here to try and keep the marauding Danes at bay and today they make a good viewpoint: north over the village to the South Downs; south to Arundel's medieval-looking castle (completed in fact in 1903); and west across a languorous loop of the River Arun and its watermeadows to a stretch of the Wey and Arun Canal, built as a short-cut in the 19th century. Flint and brick cottages, some with thatched roofs, some tiled, nestle in the trees round the squat,

The village as seen from the earthworks

flint church. St Mary's is mostly 12th- and 13th-century and has a good Norman interior, white and spacious, with exuberant carving on the pillars. It incorporates some Roman tiles and there are the remains of a Roman pavement near the north transept. Near the church is the George and Dragon, a pub with a long history of smuggling connections. From the grassy open space a footpath follows steps down to the riverbank. On the village's south-eastern outskirts, at Lea Farm on Wepham Down, there was a leper colony in the Middle Ages, from which a track south known as Lepers' Way took its name.

Old shops and cottages form an almost unbroken line in the high street

BURWASH
East Sussex

5 MILES (8 KM) EAST OF HEATHFIELD

The wealth of a bygone era is immediately recognisable in the number of prestigious old houses in Burwash, a village of exceptional beauty and harmony spread along a ridge of the Weald between the Rivers Dudwell and Rother. The soil of the Weald has always been rich in iron, and between the 15th and the 17th centuries foundries by the dozen were smelting the ore, supplying the arms and armour for the country's conquering heroes. Burwash was one of the main centres of this Wealden iron industry and some of its most striking buildings are old ironmasters' houses. The houses and cottages of the village,

timber-framed, stuccoed, mellow brick and tile-hung, are mainly in one long, wide street lined with pollarded limes. One of the best is Rampyndene, a large brick and tile-hung house with majestically tall chimneys, built in 1699 by a timber merchant. Timber merchants, of course, prospered from the iron industry too, for it depended on the oaks of the local forests – extensive at that time – for the charcoal needed for smelting. The church, which has an early Norman tower, has some early iron tomb slabs. Bateman's is a fine stone-built Jacobean house just south of the village, built in 1634 by a local ironmaster. From 1902 to 1936 it was the home of Rudyard Kipling.

Bateman's at Burwash

Rudyard Kipling and his wife bought Bateman's in 1902 and stayed there until they died, he in 1936, she in 1939. The 300 acre (122ha) estate was laid out by Mrs Kipling. Works he wrote while living here include *Puck of Pook's Hill* and the poem 'If'. Bateman's is now in the hands of the National Trust and visitors can see Kipling's rooms and study as they were in his lifetime. His 1928 Rolls Royce is on show in its garage.

Waterlilies on the village pond

CHIDDINGFOLD
Surrey

6 MILES (9.5 KM) SOUTH OF GODALMING

Sunday, 13 November 1825
We came through Chiddingfold, a very pretty place. There is a very pretty and extensive green opposite the church, and we were at the proper time of day to perceive that the modern system of education had by no means overlooked this little village. We saw the schools marching towards the church in military order.
William Cobbett, *Rural Rides*

Lying in a fold or 'forest clearing' of undulating countryside, Chiddingfold boasts all the ingredients of perfection. At one corner of its large, triangular green cluster the church, an ancient inn, a 17th-century working forge, a pond and some Georgian houses. In the 13th century this was the main centre of the forest glass industry. Introduced by the Normans and using local charcoal and sand, it supplied stained glass far and wide until the industry declined in the 17th century with competition from the Midlands and the Forest of Dean. Little glass remains here, but the church has one lancet window made up of pieces found on old glasswork sites. The churchyard, entered through a lych-gate that still has its timber coffin rest, is adrift with wild crocuses in spring. Many of the beautiful buildings around the green date from the heyday of the glass industry, notably the timber-framed, 14th-century Crown Inn, one of the oldest in England. Its exposed external beams were originally tile-hung. Other houses and cottages are brick and tile-hung. At one time cattle would have grazed on the green and watered in the pond, and stray livestock would have been impounded within the walls of the village pound that stand in the garden of Pound Cottage, just off the green.

CHILHAM
Kent

Narrow lanes climb up through Kentish hills and orchards to open out unexpectedly into Chilham's village square, one of Kent's show-pieces and often used as a film set. Chilham is used to visitors; for 350 years, after Thomas à Becket's murder, travellers used to pass through on The Pilgrims' Way from Winchester and London to his shrine in Canterbury Cathedral. Nowadays it is on the North Downs Way. Best appreciated out of season, its square is a delightfully haphazard mix of gabled, half-timbered houses, shops and inns dating from the late Middle Ages. Some were refaced in brick in the 18th century. Streets lead down from the corners, each lined with more old houses, some of them overhanging. At either end of the square are the church and the castle. St Mary's stands behind the 15th-century White Horse Inn, built of flint and stone and dominated by its Perpendicular west tower. The castle consists of a Norman keep built on Roman foundations and a Jacobean mansion built by Sir Dudley Digges, a high-ranking official of James I. The lodge gates in the square were added earlier this century, and the grounds (privately owned and not open to the public) were laid out by Charles I's gardener, John Tradescant, but reworked by 'Capability' Brown in the 18th century. Here wisteria was first grown in England.

In the church is a large monument by the prolific sculptor Francis Chantrey (1781–1841). It was his fortune that founded the art collection that is now housed in London's Tate Gallery.

Tudor houses include one with a bell-tower, named Pilgrims' Cottage

DEDHAM
Essex

6 MILES (9.5 KM) NORTH OF COLCHESTER

This part of Essex, it has been said, is 'pure Constable country: Nature with – as he loved it – the dew still upon her in undisturbed simplicity'. And what makes Dedham so special is that what Constable saw and painted in the first half of the 19th century is still what we see today. We can walk the lanes around Dedham, stand exactly where Constable stood, and see living paintings, unbroken links between nature and art. Dedham's fulling mill, featured in Constable's most famous painting of the village, was the key to its prosperity in the 16th century and its main street, lined with fine houses and some delightful old shop-fronts, is a reflection of the wealth derived from the cloth-making trade. To explore it is richly rewarding. The splendid 16th-century church is notable for its carving, particularly in the passage through the tower which features in several of Constable's paintings. Opposite is the Marlborough Head, a timber-framed corner house built in the 1430s as a cloth-merchant's house and later used by a dyer who stored his woad vats in the cellar. It became an inn in 1702. Other links with the cloth trade include Sherman's Hall, which was built as the home of a clothier and had its Classical brick façade added in the 1730s. Near the church is the old grammar school that Constable once attended.

Sherman's Hall, built for an ancestor of the American Civil War's General Sherman

Master Forger
In the north-west corner of the churchyard is buried Tom Keating, whose claim to fame – or perhaps infamy – was his ability to produce a 'Constable' at the drop of a hat. He pulled the wool over many an art critic's eye, until his forgery was exposed in the 1980s.

EAST MEON
Hampshire

5 MILES (8 KM) SOUTH-EAST OF PETERSFIELD

A view of the church, the courthouse and the village from the hill that was William of Wykeham's deer park

When William the Conqueror ordered his Domesday survey in 1086, East Meon had for some time been an important settlement and the church that the Normans built here was conceived on a grand scale from the outset. Its main builder, Bishop Walkelin, also rebuilt Winchester Cathedral. This, the most exciting village church in the county, sits in a dominating position, right under the lee of a perfectly rounded, chalk downland hill, its elaborately decorated tower topped with a lead-covered broach spire. Within, the Romanesque arches of the 12th-century cruciform structure can easily be distinguished from the only significant addition, the 13th-century south aisle. Most precious is the black Tournai marble font brought over from Belgium in 1150 and boldly carved with the story of Adam and Eve. Probably it was a gift of Henry of Blois, a patron of artists and craftsmen and Bishop of Winchester at the time. The Bishops of Winchester were lords of the manor and their courthouse stands just below the church, built by William of Wykeham in 1395 as a hunting lodge. Forge Sound is a single-aisled house of 1350, and Tudor House has origins of similar date. Most of the other buildings of this quiet and unspoilt village, tile-hung or brick, with some flint and thatch, line the banks of the infant River Meon, beloved of Izaak Walton, author of *The Compleat Angler* (1653).

A model of the village as it must have looked in the days of the Normans was made for the Domesday 900th anniversary exhibition which was held in Winchester, where *Domesday Book* was actually written. However, visitors must go to Normandy to see it now, where it is on permanent display in the Bayeux. Tapestry museum.

*The Moot Hall, once a
meeting-place for Bunyan's
followers*

ELSTOW
Bedfordshire

JUST SOUTH OF BEDFORD

Pilgrim's Start

'As I walked through the wilderness of this world, I lighted on a certain place, where was a den.' With these words John Bunyan began *The Pilgrim's Progress*. The settings for the story of Christian's journey towards salvation are often clearly based on places he knew locally. The 'den' is thought to refer to Bedford gaol.

*I*n 1660 Elstow's most famous son, John Bunyan, was taking part in the wrestling and dancing that took place on Sundays on the green, when he heard a voice from above asking 'Wilt thou leave thy sins and go to Heaven or have thy sins and go to Hell?'. Taking the first option, he became a Nonconformist preacher and thereby found himself in Bedford gaol. Here he stayed until 1672 and it was here, during another, shorter imprisonment, that he wrote *The Pilgrim's Progress*. Both this and *Holy War* are illustrated in stained glass in the church. The Norman church, a wonderful, lofty building with high arches and a large octagonal font where Bunyan and his daughters were baptised, is all that is left of a large nunnery. Once a year the nuns held a two-day fair, which gained a reputation for uproarious merry-making. Bunyan used it as the model for his 'Vanity Fair' and later Thackeray was to use it as the title of a novel. Attached to the church are the ruins of a 17th-century mansion. On the green the Moot Hall, a market hall dating from around 1500, houses a collection illustrating Bunyan's life and times. There are some fine black and white, timber-framed, overhung cottages, but Bunyan's humble tinker's home has long since gone.

FINCHINGFIELD
Essex

*T*he pond, the old brick bridge over the stream, the green with the church and a haphazard collection of cottages behind have somehow come together here to make a charming vignette, often featured on calendars. The attraction of this village lies in the delightfully unplanned manner in which the houses of differing sizes, styles and ages jostle together. Many have tiled roofs, some gabled, some with dormers, and many are plastered and colour-washed. Above the green, Finchingfield House has five barge-boarded gables, while the 18th-century coaching inn, The Fox, is pargeted. There is the red-brick Victorian school and the white Congregational chapel. The 17th-century house with four-stack chimneys by the foot-bridge was once the village workhouse and the timber-framed, white-gabled almshouses by the church, built in 1500 as the school, were later the guildhall. A passage leads through them to the church, standing up on the hill. Much of it is Norman, including the square west tower. The cupola replaces a spire which fell during a storm in 1702. Inside, look for the squares used in the medieval game of Nine Men's Morris, scratched on the south aisle window ledge. On the northern edge of the village is a white postmill and, near by, an unusual hexagonal thatched cottage stands.

One of the monuments inside the church is to William Kempe of nearby Spains Hall (d.1628) who, doing penance for falsely accusing his wife of infidelity, did not speak for seven years. For each year of his silence, it is said, he dug a pond in the grounds of his house.

The church towers over the jumble of rooftops

FINGEST
Buckinghamshire

6 MILES (9.5KM) SOUTH-WEST OF HIGH WYCOMBE

*T*ucked away in a deep, green valley in the Chilterns, Fingest has a particularly interesting Norman church. The flint and brick houses, cottages and farm buildings of the village – and, indeed, the main body of the church – are dwarfed by its large tower. It is early Norman, nearly 30ft (9m) square, with walls over 3ft (1m) thick, and most unusually has a twin-gabled roof above elaborately carved openings in the belfry. The present nave is not much narrower than the tower and is joined to it by a 12th-century arch. So large is the tower that it may originally have been the nave. The present chancel has no arch to it, being divided from the nave by a wooden screen in the 19th century, after restoration work was carried out. North of the church-yard are the remains of a palace of the Bishops of Lincoln, Buckinghamshire being at one time part of that bishopric. One of these bishops, Henry Burghersh, Bishop from 1320 to 1340, evidently was no friend of the needy and for his sins is doomed to wander the woods near by, a ghostly apparition dressed as a forester. South of the church is the 300-year-old chequered brick inn, a well-known hostelry.

The village in its setting deep among the beechwoods of the Chilterns

FULKING
West Sussex

7 MILES (11 KM) NORTH-WEST OF BRIGHTON

Flint walls and period houses line the street that has changed little in layout since the 16th century

T
he story that Fulking has to tell has much to do with sheep, the sheep that used to graze the South Downs in numbers that few of us today will remember. A stream flows down to the road from the steep escarpment behind the village and in late spring all the local shepherds would dam it up, closing the road temporarily, in order to wash their sheep before the shearing gangs set to work. At the end of the day, the shepherds and their dogs would relax in the Shepherd and Dog Inn. The springs that feed the stream used to be the village's only water supply and in Victorian times a pump-house was built beside the road to provide water, free and for ever, for the villagers of Fulking. This was used until the 1950s when mains water was brought here. The village has its pub and it has that other bastion, the shop, albeit struggling for survival like others, but it is unusual in never having had a church. Among its houses are some small architectural gems, several mentioned in *Domesday Book,* and several dating from the 15th and 16th centuries. With easy walks up on to the Downs on the old sheep paths, this is a delightful place in which to pause.

HE SENDETH SPRINGS INTO THE VALLEYS WHICH RUN AMONG THE HILLS OH THAT MEN WOULD PRAISE THE LORD FOR HIS GOODNESS!
(Inscription on the tiles of the pump-house)

GODSHILL
Isle of Wight

3 MILES (5 KM) WEST OF SHANKLIN

*I*n the summer months Godshill's high street buzzes with visitors swarming around a cluster of 'attractions' that few other villages in Britain can hope to compete with. There are two toy museums, a natural history centre, a model village and gardens, all served by tea-rooms and a pub. Just up the hill, however, as though standing a little aloof from all this tacky tourism, is the original, picture postcard Godshill. A perfect group of neat, thatched, greyish-stone cottages nestles under the tower of the 15th-century church: not without reason did this become a show village, but the cost of commercialism is dear.

The church, which celebrated its 950th anniversary in 1992, is not the first to stand on top of this, God's hill, overlooking the south of the island. The story goes that when the Saxons were preparing to build a church a mile or so away, their stones were miraculously moved in the night to the top of this hill. Taking this as an omen, they built their church here instead. The base of the present tower dates from the 14th century but the pinnacled top is 16th-century. Some of the windows and the transepts are also 14th-century, one with a plastered

wagon roof from the 15th century. But what is very special is the painting – and one wonders how many of Godshill's visitors venture up to the church to see this jewel. In the south transept is a medieval wall painting depicting Christ crucified on three leafy branches of a flowering lily. The extent of the naturalism is rare in so early a painting, and the mural is said by some to be unique in Britain. Also of interest is a large painting of Daniel in the lions' den, by Rubens or his school, that came from nearby Appuldurcombe House, seat of the Worsleys. Many of the effigies are to members of that family.

Several of the old houses in the village are stone-built and a number still have their thatched roofs. There is the stone 1826 school and a Wesleyan chapel of the 1840s. The Griffin Hotel is an attractive building, with bargeboarded gables. The Old Smithy does good trade, though no longer from blacksmithing, while the old vicarage gardens house the model village with its 1:10 scale replica of the church standing in the shadow of the real thing. So faithful a reproduction of the village is the model, that it incorporates a model of itself, a model of a model village.

The history of Godshill is linked closely to Appuldurcombe House, a Palladian-style mansion whose ruined shell can be visited a mile south. It was built in the early 1700s by Robert Worsley, whose family had long since been influential in the island. A later owner, Lord Yarborough, built the schoolhouse in the village, as well as The Griffin pub whose sign depicts the Worsley family insignia.

The church and cottages of the real Godshill, left can be seen faithfully reproduced in miniature, below

GREAT TEW
Oxfordshire

6 MILES (9.5 KM) EAST OF CHIPPING NORTON

*H*ere is a rare place. It was a work of art, a planned estate village that was the epitome of the perfect English village; but so dilapidated did it become that in 1978, in an effort to save it from total decay, it was declared a conservation area. Lucius Cary, Lord Falkland, lived here in the 17th century entertaining philosophers and poets, and built many of the cottages that still stand today. In 1808 J C Loudon was given free reign by General Stratton to prove his theory that beauty and utility are not incompatible in wholescale landscape improvement. He was against the idea, in vogue at the time, of removing any existing village out of sight and sound of the new big house, considering that the cottages and their gardens were actually an enhancement. All around the 14th-century church, the manor house, the thatched or stone-roofed cottages, the Victorian school, the pub and the green with its stocks are the evergreen trees that Loudon planted to show off to its best the rich colour of the limestone. The recent restoration work means that few cottages are now totally derelict, but with this rejuvenation has inevitably come a change of character, a loss of a certain charm. Cottages are smartened up, gardens are suburbanised, weekenders have arrived – but the village of Great Tew is brought back from near oblivion.

The characteristic rich ochre of the stone, here set off by neat thatch

Manor Farm – this wing was added on at right angles to a medieval house

---

HAMBLEDON
Hampshire

8 MILES (13 KM) NORTH OF PORTSMOUTH

It is as the 'cradle of cricket' that Hambledon will for ever be remembered. Cricket had been played for a long time before Hambledon Cricket Club was formed in about 1750, but within 20 years it had become the leading club in England and the chief authority for enforcing rules. Their moment of glory came in 1777 when, under Richard Nyren, the landlord of The Bat and Ball Inn on Broadhalfpenny Down, they beat an All England team by an innings and 168 runs. The village itself straggles along a valley bottom in wooded downland. There was a strong community here at the time of Domesday, and Henry III's granting of a licence for a weekly market in the 13th century was a boost to its prosperity. To this should be linked the extensive rebuilding of the church, incorporating into the nave the original, Saxon church. Markets continued to be held until the 17th century in the short but broad and pretty high street. In the main street Manor Farm is of particular interest, part of it being a stone, church-like 13th-century house. Some of the village houses have 16th-century origins hidden behind later façades, but most are Georgian brick, often painted, with tiled roofs and some use of flint. With inoffensive modern infill here and there, it adds up to an attractive village with a lively atmosphere.

*Then up with every glass and we'll sing a toast in chorus
The cricketers of Hambledon who played the game before us,
The stalwarts of the olden time who rolled a lonely down,
And made the king of games for men, with Hambledon the crown.*
Bruce Blunt, 'The Cricketers of Hambledon' (1929)

LITTLE GADDESDEN
Hertfordshire

6 MILES (9.5 KM) NORTH-WEST OF HEMEL HEMPSTEAD

Little Gaddesden lies on the Berkshire/Buckinghamshire border, deep in the woodlands and commons of the Chiltern Hills and bordering on the vast parklands of Ashridge House. Ashridge was originally built as a College of Bonshommes by the Normans but was suppressed at the dissolution and subsequently sold. It remained in the possession of the Earls of Bridgewater until bought by the National Trust in 1947. In 1808 Ashridge was rebuilt by James and Jeffry Wyatt on a colossal scale, in sumptuous Gothic Revival style. Little Gaddesden dates mainly from the 16th century when the monastic buildings were turned into a large house at the centre of a huge estate. A 'B' and a coronet can be seen on many of the houses, showing that they were estate workers' cottages. The village is basically one street, with houses and cottages straggling along one side only, set back from the road behind a broad stretch of grass. John O'Gaddesden's House, named after the 14th-century royal physician, is a delightful timber-framed, pargeted house of the 15th century. The stone-built manor house, dated 1576, has two turrets with stepped gables. The village church, interesting only for its monuments, is half a mile away from the houses. Its isolation, together with the existence of various humps and bumps near by, suggest a deserted village.

Timber-framed Manor Cottage

Memorial
The Ashridge Estate covers some 4000 acres (1620ha) of woodlands and commons and is open to the public. A focal point is the granite monument erected in the middle of the 19th century to the 3rd Duke of Bridgewater, the 'Canal Duke', who commissioned James Brindley to build England's first canal from his Worsley coal mines to Manchester. It opened in 1761.

PLESHEY
Essex

6 MILES (9.5 KM) NORTH-WEST OF CHELMSFORD

One of the picturesque row of cottages beneath the castle mound

The whole of Pleshey village stands most evocatively within the earthworks of an important castle built in the 12th century by the Norman Geoffrey de Mandeville. Approach the village from the east, cross the outer bailey and the lane becomes the village high street. The vast, flat-topped mound can take one by surprise, rising up suddenly and dramatically behind the cottages, 60ft (18m) high and 300ft (91m) across at its base. The castle that stood on top was home for over 200 years to successive Lords High Constable of England before coming to Richard II's uncle, Thomas Duke of Gloucester. Gloucester founded a college of priests here in 1393 and the crossing arches of the building (but nothing else) are still to be seen within the church, extensively rebuilt in 1868. The only building preserved from the castle is the 15th-century brick bridge linking the mound with the inner bailey. It is said that, in 1558, when Queen Elizabeth's Commissioners discovered that the villagers were keeping rabbits in the castle ruins and this was their only means of access over the moat, they allowed it to remain. Walk across it on to the mound for wide-stretching views over the trees and attractive houses of the village to the farmlands of Essex.

SELBORNE
Hampshire

4 MILES (6.5 KM) SOUTH OF ALTON

Selborne was immortalised in 1789 by the publication of Reverend Gilbert White's *The Natural History and Antiquities of Selborne*. Since then his gentle, humorous and meticulous observations of life in the gardens, fields, hedgerows and woodlands around Selborne have become a favourite classic of country writing that has seen more than 200 editions. Gilbert White was born here in 1720, spent most of his life here as curate, and died in The Wakes in 1793, being buried in the churchyard. His gravestone is so simple it is easy to miss, bearing at his own request the plain inscription 'G W 26th June 1793'. Inside the church there is a window dedicated to him, alive with birds,

The village, seen from The Hanger

The Wakes, Gilbert White's home

Selborne, 9 September 1767
I was much entertained last summer with a tame bat, which would take flies out of a person's hand. If you gave it anything to eat, it brought its wings round before the mouth, hovering and hiding its head in the manner of birds of prey when they feed.

18 April 1768
The fly-catcher has not yet appeared: it usually breeds in my vine. The redstart begins to sing: its note is short and imperfect, but is continued till about the middle of June. The willow-wrens (the smaller sort) are horrid pests in a garden, destroying the pease, cherries, currants, etc.

1 August 1771
A neighbour of mine, who is said to have a nice ear, remarks that the owls about this village hoot in three different keys, in G flat, or F sharp, in B flat and A flat. He heard two hooting to each other, the one in A flat, and the other in B flat. Query: Do these different notes proceed from different species, or only from various individuals?

22 November 1777
This sudden summer-like heat was attended by many summer coincidences; for on those two days the thermometer rose to sixty-six in the shade; many species of insects revived and came forth; some bees swarmed in this neighbourhood; the old tortoise . . . awakened and came forth out of his dormitory.

(Observations from Gilbert White's *The Natural History of Selborne*)

animals and flowers. There is also a beautiful Flemish 16th-century triptych depicting the Adoration of the Magi. Some alterations to the partly Norman, partly Perpendicular church were made in 1856 by Gilbert White's great nephew. The famous Selborne yew, 35ft (10.5m) in girth, was nearly 1400 years old when it was blown down in a gale in January 1990. Sadly, it failed to survive when replanted, but a cutting taken from it now grows opposite the west door. Through the churchyard a path leads across watermeadows to the woods of Short Lythe and Long Lythe, National Trust land. Remains of a 13th-century Augustinian priory have been found near by.

Immediately adjoining the churchyard is The Plestor, the small village green, edged with old houses and sloping down to the road that goes right through the village. Near by, on this road, is The Wakes, White's home. Later it was the home of gallant Captain Oates, of Antarctic fame. The Wakes now houses a museum devoted to White and Oates. Behind the house is the garden Gilbert White so loved. On the other side of the road from the house can be seen the trees White planted to screen the blood and gore of the butcher's shop opposite. The houses and cottages along this, the main artery of the village, are mostly old and pleasant, brick and tiled, but not particularly distinguished.

Behind the Selborne Arms is the path that leads to the Zig-Zag, a path cut by Gilbert and his brother in 1753 that winds up the steep slope of The Hanger to the beechwoods and common at the top, also National Trust land. From the seat at the top there are far-reaching views over the rooftops of Selborne to the South Downs. Paths lead back down to the village.

The butcher's shop in a high street that has shown little change over the centuries

---

❊

SMARDEN
Kent

10 MILES (16 KM) WEST OF ASHFORD

❊

In the summer of 1450, 66 weavers, fullers, drapers and tailors from Smarden joined hundreds of other men from Kent under the leadership of one Jack Cade and marched to London to protest at unreasonably high taxes and prices. After some fierce altercation, concessions were made and most of the men went home, but Cade was hunted down by the Government and killed.

*A*n old Wealden wool village, Smarden has a particularly attractive high street, with white weatherboarded and half-timbered houses on either side. The Dragon House, next to the village pump, was built in 1331 for a family of Dutch weavers brought over by Edward III to weave broadcloth. Chessenden is a good Wealden hall house, built in 1462. Further evidence of the village's prosperity as a cloth town is to be found near the church in the two big half-timbered houses built by wealthy clothiers. The excellent cloth hall is dated to about 1420; the hoist that was used for lifting bales of cloth into the loft still hangs from the gable at the west end.

Next door, Matthew Hartnup's house has his name carved on it; it is probably older than the 1671 date shown. The church dates from the 14th century, with a 15th-century tower, and is built of local Bethersden marble. It is called the 'Barn of Kent' because of its surprising width and absence of aisles to support the 36ft (11m) span of its wooden roof, a rare occurrence in medieval churches. Another rarity is the oven for baking communion wafers, near the high altar. Smarden continued to thrive as a weaving town, with a weekly market, until the 19th century when hops were introduced to the area. Oast houses in the village date from this time.

THAXTED
Essex

7 MILES (11 KM) SOUTH-EAST OF SAFFRON WALDEN

Not only can Thaxted claim the most glorious church in Essex, it also boasts a most magnificent ancient guildhall. And, as if that were not enough, it has an uncommon wealth of other historic buildings. In the Middle Ages Thaxted became an important centre for the cutlery trade. There is no iron in the vicinity so it may have been that knives and swords were brought here for finishing. The guildhall, built by the cutlers in about 1400, stands at the centre of the village, a proud three-storey building, each floor overhanging the one below. All around it are more 15th-century timber-framed and overhanging buildings, some with pargeting. Other houses were medieval in origin and have Georgian plasterwork façades; a number date wholly from the Georgian period, by which time the cutlery trade had declined and Thaxted was a more modest market centre. All blend together most harmoniously. From the guildhall a narrow lane leads up to the church. Its spire soars over the buildings below in proclamation of the wealth of its medieval builders, the cutlers and the lords of the manor, the de Clares. There are some beautiful details externally, while the inside is light and airy. Near the church is a double row of almshouses, one thatched, with a view between them of Thaxted's disused tower windmill.

Gustav Holst, the composer, lived next to the Recorder's house in Town Street from 1917 to 1925, working mainly on comic operas and choral pieces.

The cutlers' guildhall

WEST WYCOMBE
Buckinghamshire

2 MILES (3 KM) NORTH-WEST OF HIGH WYCOMBE

The whole of West Wycombe is owned by the National Trust. In 1929 the Dashwood family put the house, park and village up for sale in 60 lots. The Royal Society of Arts, in a move to prevent the break-up of an estate village that had hardly changed since the 17th century, stepped in to buy the whole package. After sympathetic repair work, they handed it to the National Trust in 1934.

The village seen from the hill where Dashwood's mausoleum stands

By the time the Dashwood family acquired the estate of West Wycombe in 1698, the village had long since grown used to the traffic that passed through on the road from London to Oxford and beyond, and at the height of the coaching age there were eight coaching inns here. It was the activities of the second Sir Francis Dashwood in the 18th century, however, which really put the place on the map. Founder of the Society of Dilettanti and an altogether ravishingly eccentric character, he is notorious for his Hell Fire Club connections. It was he who had the Palladian house built and the park landscaped (by Humphry Repton), during the course of which he had the main road diverted from the village. The quarrying of chalk for the new road created the Caves, which were used for Hell Fire meetings. Above them is his folly of a mausoleum, and the church he had almost completely rebuilt to reflect his love of things Italian. Under the golden orb on top of the tower, it is said, he held parties. The delightful village remains much as he inherited it. A few Georgian, brick or flint houses are interspersed between the small, timber-framed 16th-century houses. Arches lead into the courtyards of the old coaching inns, while Church Lane is entered beneath Church Loft, a medieval pilgrims' hospice.

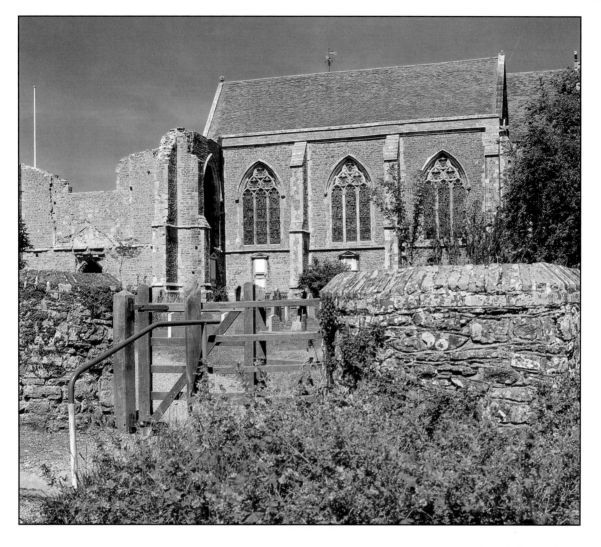

WINCHELSEA
East Sussex

10 MILES (16 KM) EAST OF HASTINGS

St Thomas's Church, planned on a vast scale but never completed

'New' Winchelsea stands on a hill, well above the sea that in the 13th century drowned the original Winchelsea, the town that had joined the confederation of Cinque Ports in 1191. The new town was built by Edward I to replace the old, as a defensive port and centre for the wine trade with France. But the sea is a law unto itself and before long it receded, leaving Winchelsea stuck on the marshes, a mile inland. Its harbour silted up and trading collapsed, the French kept raiding, the Black Death swept through and Winchelsea went into decline. Similar fates befell other places but what is so individual is its layout. Within defensive walls that have survived in part to this day, Edward I used a grid pattern for the streets and although his buildings have mostly gone, the plan remains. Three of the 14th-century town gates guard the entrances, and the 14th-century chancel of the Church of St Thomas, all that was ever finished, survives, complete with a contemporary wall-painting and monuments. Medieval wine vaults can be seen beneath some of the inns, and the court house, now a museum, is a reminder of the days of prosperity – but mostly it is red-roofed houses, tile-hung and white-painted, that line the chequerboard streets of this peaceful and beautiful village.

Winchelsea and Rye

An historic patina covers their buildings more deeply than any others, in England at least. Indeed, I know of no place save for Paris, where memories seem so thick on every stone.
Ford Madox Ford, *Return to Yesterday* (1932)

A Norfolk village sign which says it all

CENTRAL ENGLAND AND EAST ANGLIA

*The slopes of wold and valley are dotted with copses and
noble trees, amongst which lie tiny villages and square-
towered churches...Beyond the eastern range of hills lies
the marsh, a flat strip of rich pasture land about five to
eight miles wide, divided up into fields by broad ditches,
which are filled in summer with tall, feathery reeds.
Beyond this is the North Sea, peculiar for the long rise
and fall of the tide over the flat sandy shore and fringed by
a line of high sand dunes...*

Charles Tennyson,
describing the Lincolnshire landscape near
Somersby, birthplace of his grandfather,
Alfred Lord Tennyson

Ancient Rites
The antlers used for the Horn
Dance have been carbon dated
to Norman times but, although
the dance seems to have been
connected with the church
since medieval days, there are
elements that suggest much
earlier, pre-Christian rituals.
Maid Marian, a man dressed
as a woman, for example, hints
at ancient fertility rites, while
the bowman stalking the deer
men is reminiscent of a Stone
Age painting in the Lascaux
Caves depicting bowmen in
pursuit of men wearing antlers
on their heads.

ABBOTS BROMLEY
Staffordshire

5 MILES (8 KM) NORTH-EAST OF RUGELEY

*I*t is for its ancient Horn Dance, performed early in September, that the name of Abbots Bromley is familiar to many. But the village has plenty to beguile the visitor in other months too, particularly enthusiasts of timber-framing. At the centre of this one-time market town the hexagonal butter cross building marks where local farmers used to trade their produce. Close by is the black and white panelled Goat's Head Inn and the brick-built Bagot Almshouses, endowed in 1705 by the local family who have lived for 500 years in nearby Blithfield Hall. The public school, St Mary and St Anne's, is housed in a clump of buildings behind the lofty 1881 chapel on the high street, while the village school house of 1606 is another half-timbered building, behind a Victorian successor in Schoolhouse Lane. In a number of houses timber-framing is concealed behind brick, but there is nothing to hide the glory of Church House, whose particularly fanciful timberwork is typical of the West Midlands. The church is restored medieval, and it is here that the reindeer horns used for the Horn Dance are kept. Six deer men carry the horns and perform this ancient ritual, of uncertain origin, in and around the village, accompanied by a fool, a hobby horse, a bowman and the man-woman, Maid Marian.

The butter cross and the Goat's Head Inn

One of the old stone cottages grouped contentedly together in the heart of the village

---

AYNHO
Northamptonshire

6 MILES (9.5 KM) SOUTH-EAST OF BANBURY

River, canal, railway and now motorway twist their way like plaited ribbons along the Cherwell valley below this hilly, limestone village. In its early days it was fortified; todayit has some enticing and rewarding nooks and crannies to explore. The church dates from the 14th century and there may even have been a settlement here before the Normans, but most of the notable buildings in the village date from the 17th century onwards, when the Cartwright family bought the manor here. It is said that they used to claim the rent from their tenants in the form of apricots, and to this day a number of apricot trees can be seen growing on sunny house fronts. Apricots like the local limestone soil. During the Civil War, in 1645, Royalist troops burnt the Cartwrights' house down, but they had it rebuilt, and at about the same time the church too was rebuilt to match it. It is symmetrical, two-storeyed, and looks like a grand house. The old grammar school is a fine building, dated to 1671, and near by are the two-storeyed almshouses built in 1822. There are lovely grey-gold limestone houses and cottages everywhere. Opposite the old coaching inn, The Cartwright Arms, by the green, is the village hall built with stone from the medieval pesthouse where plague victims were isolated.

There is a story that in 1646 Robert Wylde applied for the post of rector here. He and the other applicant were required to preach a sermon, after which a vote was taken. When asked the result, Wylde is said to have replied that it was divided: ' I got the Ay, he the No.'

Sheep graze peacefully below Beeby's Tub

BEEBY
Leicestershire

5 MILES (8 KM) NORTH-EAST OF LEICESTER

In summer's heat and winter's cold
One constant temperature I hold.
When brooks and wells and rivers dry
I always yield a full supply.
My neighbours say (I'm often told)
I'm more than worth my weight in gold.
(Inscription in stone on the village well)

'Beeby's Tub' is unlikely nomenclature for a church spire. It certainly suggests there may be a story to tell. And, indeed, there are several legends attached to this stump of a spire that squats unfinished on the handsome ironstone tower of All Saints' Church, Beeby. One explanation is that the builder felt he could never compete with the highly decorative spire of nearby Queniborough Church, and threw himself off in despair. Another story is that the builders were brothers who had a quarrel up there. One pushed the other to his death from the battlements, and then felt such remorse that he too jumped, following his brother to his grave.

Or maybe the money just ran out. This rather fine church is no longer used for services but is being maintained by the Redundant Churches' Fund. Near it the Victorians erected a cover over the well that would have been the villagers' water supply for many centuries. Certainly there is evidence of a pre-Norman village which was deserted in the Middle Ages. The church stands beside a field, cut by a stream and shaded by an old Wellingtonia. Also here are The Manor House, The Grange, an old, beautifully restored yeoman farmhouse and some brick cottages which once housed a brewery. Stray hops still grow in the hedges of this tiny, peaceful place.

BERKSWELL
West Midlands

6 MILES (9.5 KM) WEST OF COVENTRY

Berk, or as he was known to the Anglo Saxons Bercol, owned a well here in the Forest of Arden, in which the King of the Mercians was baptised by the monks of Lichfield. This large square stone well is behind the brick, Victorian almshouses that face the green. The king went on to build a small church here, providing it with a large crypt. When the Normans rebuilt the church in the 12th century, they reconstructed this crypt and built another one alongside. They are exceptional. There is a very good Norman chancel, a monument by Westmacott decorated with roses and voluptuous angels, and several woodcarver-Thompson mouse trademarks. Outside, the south doorway is sheltered by a half-timbered porch with a room over, its grey timbers set off by the pinkish sandstone walls of this lovely church. The adjoining 17th-century old rectory is stone-faced and has prettily shaped gables. There is some thatch and some timber-framing in the village, including the 400-year-old Bear Inn outside which stands a cannon from the Crimean War. On the green itself are the old stocks. Why do they have five holes, is the puzzle. Was it to accommodate a particular one-legged reprobate alongside his two mates? Or, perhaps, has a sixth hole rotted away?

A hobby horse is, unexpectedly, housed in the church porch. It is said to have been used by an 18th-century huntsman parson who felt able to preach only when on horseback.

In a village that once supported a brick-making industry, mellow brick walls are a foil to a pretty cottage garden

BURNHAM THORPE
Norfolk

6 MILES (9.5 KM) WEST OF WELLS-NEXT-THE-SEA

This is the birthplace of Horatio Nelson. Burnham Thorpe is quietly proud of its son, England's greatest naval hero, but has never allowed itself to be degraded by any sort of souvenir industry. The pub and the church have plenty of Nelson memorabilia, but elsewhere the old flint village seems to carry on with life quite ordinarily. The Lord Nelson looks much as it must have done when he held a party here before setting off on HMS *Agamemnon* to fight Napoleon – except, that is, for the publican's admirable collection of Nelsonia. Next door is a handsome flint barn, probably a warehouse when the stream beside it was a tidal, navigable river. Locals say that Nelson's mother gave birth to him here, being unable to make it home to the rectory in time. The official story is that he was born, in 1758, in the old rectory, the site of which is marked with a plaque. A little north of the village centre is the church where Horatio's father was parson. The lectern and cross are made from timber from HMS *Victory*, and flags from the ship hang in the nave. The church itself dates from the 13th century. Do not miss the beautiful decorative flintwork on the exterior of the east wall.

The flint walling of a cottage in the village, typical of this part of Norfolk

The Nelson Connection
The village is only a few miles from the north Norfolk coast, off which Nelson may have learnt to sail as a young boy. He joined the navy in 1770, aged 12, and served in the Arctic, the East and West Indies and in North American waters during the War of Independence.
In 1788 he was back here again, with his wife Fanny, farming to supplement his half-pay for the five years until war broke out with France.

The Peddars Way is a Roman track that may well have been built on the route of an even more ancient, Celtic track. It is now a long-distance path that runs from Knettishall Heath, just over the Suffolk border, north-west to Holme next the Sea. Castle Acre is the only village of note as it makes its way across the Breckland and the remote north-west corner of Norfolk.

The 11th-century Bailey Gate at Castle Acre

CASTLE ACRE
Norfolk

4 MILES (6.5 KM) NORTH OF SWAFFHAM

Castle Acre is a good stopping-off place for walkers on the ancient Peddars Way. The Normans, however, did more than break their journey here. They built in a big way, and the ruins we are left with now are some of the most evocative in the land. William the Conqueror's son-in-law, William de Warenne, built a huge castle within the outer bailey of which much of today's village stands. Apart from the strikingly massive earthworks, little but its gateway remains. However, in 1090 Warenne built a Cluniac priory here and it is for this rather than the castle that Castle Acre is known. It was damaged badly in the dissolution, but one look at its soaring west front and the intricate decoration of its blind arcading and it takes only a little imagination to visualise what a thing of splendour this must have been. The Prior's Lodging is the only part of the building to have kept a roof. Many of the brick-and-flint houses of the village are built of material from the castle and priory ruins (both of which are in the care of English Heritage). Some buildings are new, many are 19th-century, one or two are medieval and the Ostrich Inn is 18th-century. Everything pulls together to make this a most attractive place.

Pargeting, the art of raised (or occasionally incised) decorative plasterwork, is quite commonly seen on façades and gables of timber-framed houses in the towns and larger villages of Suffolk, Essex and Hertfordshire. The technique, developed in the 16th and 17th centuries, was to *pour jeter* (throw) plaster over the timber-framing. Patterns were then applied by pressing moulds into it while it was still wet. Earlier examples usually depict plants, animals or people, while later designs tend to be more geometric.

The Ancient House, a former priest's house next to the church, is dated 1473 – its pargeting would have been added much later

CLARE
Suffolk

7 MILES (11 KM) WEST OF SUDBURY

*I*n the streets at the centre of this substantial village are many beautiful old houses, cottages and shops, some dating back to the 15th century. A number are exquisite examples of the local art of pargeting, the plasterwork patterning on their frontages bringing to mind delicately embroidered linen or an intricately iced cake. Like so many villages in this part of the country, Clare is a legacy of the enormous prosperity that came from the woollen cloth trade in the Middle Ages. Its origins, however, are in its Iron Age hillfort, near the church. Later, the Norman de Clare family, recognising its commanding position over the Stour valley, built a motte and bailey here which was to become the centre of the powerful empire known as the Honour of Clare. In 1248 Gilbert de Clare built an Augustinian priory on the banks of the river, the first of that order in England. It was dissolved in 1538, but in 1954 the monks returned and Clare is an Augustinian priory once more. The big flint church above the market place dates in part from the 13th century. Its medieval stained glass was mostly smashed in 1643 by the Puritan William Dowsing, who went about East Anglia destroying 'pictures superstitious'. He left the heraldic pieces; he had no problems, presumably, with heraldry.

The old forge

CLAVERDON
Warwickshire

6 MILES (9.5 KM) WEST OF WARWICK

*C*laverdon, or Clover Down, is an ancient village set on a hill overlooking the Warwickshire countryside. With its ready access to the M40, its attractions are not lost on Birmingham commuters but it has retained a sense of community and there are several good old buildings. The church, of greyish stone, was built in the 15th century but partly reconstructed during the 19th century. Here is the tomb of Sir Thomas Spencer (*d*.1630), lord of the manor. His house was demolished some 30 years after his death, though the stone tower-house of the Hall is said to have been part of it. Also in the church is a tablet commemorating Francis Galton, FRS (1822–1911), grandson of Erasmus Darwin and cousin of Charles. He studied heredity and it was he who established that fingerprints are permanent and unique. He was also the first to construct serious weather charts. There are a number of timber-framed buildings, some 16th-century, including Park Farm and its cottages. The mid-19th-century school buildings (now private housing), in contrast, have an Italianate air. The most unusual building in the village has to be the old forge, a half-timbered building with a uniquely fitting doorway.

CLEY NEXT THE SEA
Norfolk

Cley is one of a string of old flint villages threaded like beads along Norfolk's north coast. It is a small, quiet place, a mile or so across the marshes that now lie between it and the sea, but its large 18th-century Customs House on the old quay is indicative of the volume of trade that was carried on with the Continent before the River Glaven silted up. Also on the former quayside is Cley's great five-storey windmill, now a guesthouse with some self-catering apartments which looks out over the saltmarshes that are a nature reserve. The village originally was centred on the church but after a fire in the 17th century new houses were built in the quayside area, leaving the church standing apart on Newgate Green. Most of the pretty brick-and-flint houses and cottages open directly on to the main street that winds through the village. The church was largely rebuilt in the prosperous days of the 14th century when Cley was exporting thousands of tons of raw wool. It has a beautiful south porch, a wonderful nave and some excellent carvings and brasses. The transepts have been in ruins since about 1600 and it never had a west tower; it seems the Black Death, or perhaps the shift of prosperity away from ports dealing in raw wool to weaving centres further south, dealt a blow to that.

The rooftops of Cley – Dutch gables are a reflection of trading contacts with the Low Countries

CROMFORD
Derbyshire

2 MILES (3 KM) SOUTH OF MATLOCK

The Arkwright Society is involved in major restoration work on this, the first cotton mill in the country

This is Richard Arkwright's village, and the place where the factory system was born at the beginning of the Industrial Revolution. Once he had invented the spinning machine, Arkwright went on to build England's first cotton mill, in 1771, in the beautiful Derwent valley. The huge mill building still stands, close to a medieval bridge over the river whose waters Arkwright chose to power his machines. His wharves and storage buildings are ranged beside the canal that was constructed in 1793 to link his mill with the major cities of the North and the Midlands. He also built cottages to house his workers, the best examples being in North Street

– austere terraces of solid, three-storeyed gritstone houses, the top floors of which were probably used as workshops. Smaller cottages, also gritstone, climb Cromford Hill away from the river. In the centre of the village he built The Greyhound Inn. Near the bridge is the church he built in 1797. It was gothicised by the Victorians. He also provided chapels and a Sunday school, creating a complete new village for the workforce in what had been until then an unpopulated location. On the other side of the Derwent, in proud position to admire his works, is his own house, Willersley Castle, which sadly he did not see completed before he died in 1792.

The dawning of the Industrial Revolution was seen by contemporaries to exemplify man's triumphs over nature, and these early feats were often the subject of painting or poetry. Erasmus Darwin wrote of Cromford, 'where Derwent guides his dusky floods/ Through vaulted mountains and a night of woods', inspired not only by the picturesque situation of Arkwright's first mill but also by the industrial architecture and the innovative machinery it housed. It is only with our hindsight that we see countryside devastated in the name of progress.

EYAM
Derbyshire

12 MILES (19 KM) NORTH-WEST OF CHESTERFIELD

*I*t was in one of the houses near the church, known as Plague Cottages, that in September 1665 the village tailor took delivery of a box of clothes from London that was contaminated with plague germs. The deadly disease spread rapidly through the village, the people panicked and prepared to leave. But their parson, William Mompesson, encouraged them to stay, bravely isolating the place from the outside world in order to prevent the disease spreading across the county. The heroic villagers paid dearly for their courage, for out of some 350 inhabitants, 259 died. Whole families were wiped out; the graves of one entire family, the Rileys, can be seen to the west of the village. Mompesson closed the church and held services in the open air in The Delph. His wife was one of the victims and her grave may be seen in the churchyard. Despite reminders of its sad past, Eyam (pronounced 'Eem') is none the less one of the Peak District's most pleasing villages. It has a good variety of houses built solidly, in the 17th and 18th centuries, in local gritstone and in traditional Peakland styles. Some border the square, others line the sloping main street. Beside the church is a Saxon cross, its cross-head, unusually, still intact. The ancient tradition of well-dressing is practised here.

One of the row of six Plague Cottages, with its poignant reminder of their sad past

The River Great Ouse, in whose waters, it is said, lies the church spire

HEMINGFORD GREY
Cambridgeshire

3 MILES (5 KM) EAST OF GODMANCHESTER

The banks of the River Great Ouse make a pretty setting for a lovely village, and in particular for a very special manor house. This is the oldest continuously inhabited house in England. In about 1130 its Norman owner built a two-storeyed house consisting of a storeroom on the ground floor and a hall above, entered by an outside staircase. The original Norman windows survive, as does a huge fireplace inside. The garden is bounded by the river on one side and a moat on the other three. The hall has been added to over the ages, but it remains a quite enchanted place and its last owner, Lucy Boston, used it as the setting of her classic *Green Knowe*

children's novels. Twelfth-century Norman stonework also survives in the solid round pillars in the north arcade of the village church. Other parts of the building date from the 13th century, including the beautiful double piscina with intersecting arches and mouldings. Outside, one cannot fail to notice the oddly truncated spire on top of the buttressed tower. Unlike Beeby's (see page 74), this spire was finished, but was blown down by a storm in 1741. The stump was then topped by decorative ball finials. There is a morass of undistinguished modern housing in the village, but at its heart are several striking houses of the 16th to 18th centuries.

Joseph came to a little sunlit place where there were yew bushes cut into the shapes of chess men. The castles had battlements round the top. With constant clipping the walls were solid... There was a door in the bastion... He felt a passionate longing to go in. (The garden of the manor house, described by Lucy Boston in *The Castle of Yew* (1965). The house and garden are open by appointment.)

ILMINGTON
Warwickshire

4 MILES (6.5 KM) NORTH-WEST OF SHIPSTON ON STOUR

A tangle of lanes and alleyways, golden houses with mullioned windows and stone roofs, old cottage gardens, far-reaching views – even Morris dancing. Ilmington has everything needed to make it one of the county's show pieces; it is in that part of Warwickshire that seems to jab cheekily into Gloucestershire and Oxfordshire and shares all the Cotswold hallmarks. There is a chalybeate spring, which in the late 19th century turned the place into something of a spa for a while. A large pool at the northern end of the village is the site of fish ponds which belonged to the manor opposite. The manor was built in the 16th century with fine gables and mullioned windows looking on to its lovely garden. Footpaths lead to the church below the upper green. It has a chunky Norman tower and zig-zagged doorway. Inside, it feels wide, with hefty arches to the tower and chancel. The Victorian old school building, with bell-cote, is now a Roman Catholic church, while at the western end of the upper green is stone-built Crab Mill, dated to 1711. Facing on to the lower of the two greens is the shop and The Howard Inn, named after one of the leading families of the area who lived in Foxcote House, an early Georgian mansion a little out of the village.

Summer sunshine brings out the warmth of the Cotswold stone

Great Gardens
Just 2 or 3 miles away, over the border with Gloucestershire, are two glorious Cotswold gardens, Hidcote Manor Garden (National Trust), a series of small gardens created by the great horticulturist Lawrence Johnston, and Kiftsgate Court Garden, noted for its collection of old-fashioned roses. Both are open to the public from spring to autumn.

A colour-washed corner of a village so unique that it is best explored out of season

KERSEY
Suffolk

10 MILES (16 KM) WEST OF IPSWICH

Kersey, all of it, is just one street that runs down from its church on top of one hill, to a watersplash through a little river, and then steeply up again the other side to the ruins of a priory that crowned the hill opposite. From either end there is one of the most enchanting views to be found in Suffolk, across the red-tiled gables and rooftops of the ancient half-timbered houses. Many of the houses are pastel colour-washed, all leaning out and in and up against one another. The watersplash provided the running water needed for washing the Kersey cloth produced here in the late Middle Ages and every house was either the home of a cloth merchant or a weaver's cottage, in which there would have been a loom at work – this was literally a cottage industry. The church was built largely in the 14th century on this wealth, big and beautifully decorated within and without. Outside, there is ornate flint flushwork; the inside got beaten up a bit in the Reformation but some lovely things survive. By the stream is a 500-year-old house with a huge timber-framed doorway; in The Green are chocolate-box, pastel cottages; while opposite The White Horse is a group of timber-framed houses, with worn steps leading up to old oak doors and ancient bay windows.

The Swan Inn used to be a favourite of the American airmen of the 487th Bomb Group who were based in the area during World War II. It has a collection of wartime memorabilia and in one bar preserves a section of wall that is covered with the airmen's signatures.

Timber-frame construction in East Anglia is different from that of other areas in that many more vertical timbers are used than horizontal. The verticals are therefore placed quite close together, producing a totally different effect from the square chequerboard frontages seen in Cheshire or the Midlands. Notable by their absence in East Anglia are cruck and jointed-cruck trusses, used in every area of the country except the eastern counties.

Little Hall, home of the Suffolk Preservation Society and the Gayer-Anderson Collection of paintings, ceramics and furniture

LAVENHAM
Suffolk

6 MILES (9.5 KM) NORTH-EAST OF SUDBURY

*T*his is the most famous, the most glorious, of all Suffolk's famous and glorious wool villages. In 1326 Edward III banned the import of foreign cloth, giving a boost to home industry and encouraging the immigration into East Anglia of Flemish weavers with whom there were already trading connections.

Through the 14th and 15th centuries Lavenham developed and prospered, rebuilding itself in appropriately wealthy style. After about 1600, however, little new building took place as Lavenham, along with other wool towns, began to decline. With the development of water-power for the fulling process, the weaving industry began to shift towards the hill streams of the west and north of England, and with the invention of the power loom dependent on water and then coal, weaving in East Anglia was finished. Lavenham reverted to agriculture and never became industrialised. The magnificent timbered cloth-halls, the fine cloth-merchants' houses, the beautiful guildhall, the quite splendid church, even the weavers' cottages have more or less all remained intact. Somehow, it is as though time has stood still for those medieval weavers and dyers and fullers.

To walk about Lavenham is to breathe its medieval perfection through every pore. Sailing above the village and the undulating countryside that nourished it is the great knapped flint church tower. This is a most spectacular church, built on the combined funds of a rich clothier, Thomas Spring, and the de Veres, Earls of Oxford. The interior is elaborate; of its finer detailing note, if nothing else, the charming carvings

on the misericords (the pelican, especially) and the amazingly elaborate Spring family pew. They and their fellow cloth-merchants would have operated from the early 16th-century guildhall. Look closely at the exceptional quality of the decoration of its timbering and it is clear that Lavenham was no run-of-the-mill place. Notice particularly the carved corner posts of the porch. Also in the market place is Little Hall, another beautiful half-timbered building of the 14th century, the 500-year-old Angel Hotel and some Georgian remodelled frontages. The market cross has stood since 1501. The Swan Hotel now incorporates the old wool hall, another superb timbered building. But there are superb timbered buildings in every street, round every corner. Gables lean in or out, jetties slope up or down, roofs dip and rise. Suddenly a little carved head peeks out from under an eave. It has watched countless generations go by. It has always been there, one feels, and it surely always will be.

The 16th-century guildhall

*Old fishermen's cottages in
Quay Street, which in Tudor
times was under the sea*

ORFORD
Suffolk

9 MILES (14.5 KM) EAST OF WOODBRIDGE

Musical Premières

Several of Benjamin Britten's works had their first performances in the broad, lofty nave of Orford Church, notably *Noye's Fludde* (1958), based on the Chester miracle play and intended by the composer for performance in church with the audience participating in traditional hymns; and three one-act Church Parables, *Curlew River* (1964), *The Burning Fiery Furnace* (1968) and *The Prodigal Son* (1968).

Glance at a map or, better, look east from the top of the castle keep. Between Orford and the sea lie first the River Ore and then the 10-mile-long (16km) shingle bank of Orford Ness. This began to build up in the 16th century, gradually silting up the river and rendering the harbour useless for trade. Hence Orford's decline from a busy medieval port trading in wool with access to the open sea – and three churches, two hospitals and a friary – to today's pleasant and peaceful village of brick and timber-framing with a riverside quay popular with pleasure craft. Its castle keep, however, has stood oblivious to the vagaries of the Suffolk coast, since

Henry II had it built in 1165–7. There are two significant things about the castle (English Heritage). It was the first to be built with a keep that was cylindrical internally and 18-sided externally, the polygonal shape making it stronger and more easily defended than a square or rectangular one. Secondly, the financial records of the King's Exchequer, the Pipe Rolls, exist, meaning that this is the oldest castle for which there is documentary evidence. The ruined chancel of the village church is of similar date, the nave and tower being 14th-century. Especially attractive are the old market square and the street that leads down to the quay.

SWAFFHAM PRIOR
Cambridgeshire

5 MILES (8 KM) WEST OF NEWMARKET

Twin churches sitting in tandem, diagonally placed in exact parallel across the square of one small churchyard: quite how this unusual phenomenon came about is a subject of speculation. Are they testimony to the rival endowments of two lords of the manor? Or, as some say, two embittered sisters? St Cyriac's dates from the 13th century but was rebuilt, except for the tower, early in the 19th century. It fell into decay but is now restored for use as a social centre, though for a time, when St Mary's spire was struck by lightning in 1767, this was in use and St Mary's was closed. St Mary's is more exciting, and particularly its tower. At its base it is very square Norman, next is an octagonal stage, also Norman, and then it goes 16-sided; all very powerful. Inside is an arresting series of early 20th-century stained-glass scenes depicting a World War I trench, an ammunition factory, Wicken Fen, and a Swiss mountain. The village street below the churchyard consists mainly of neat cottages and Georgian houses. Swaffham Prior House is mid-18th-century, of yellowish brick, while Baldwin Manor, on the outskirts, is a very lovely Tudor half-timbered house. The village also boasts two recently restored windmills, one of which turns again.

St Mary's tower – a fibreglass spire replaces the original, which fell in the 18th century

The Devil's Dyke

Just to the north-east of the village the road comes to the Devil's Dyke, a colossal Romano-British or Anglo Saxon earthwork. The bank and the ditch are 40yds (36m) wide, from the top of the bank to the bottom of the ditch it is 60ft (18m), and the total length is 7 miles (11km). Walk along it (the Devil's Dyke Morris Men choose to dance the distance) and you will appreciate that that is a lot of earth to move with your pick-axe and shovel.

Down by the river, near the bridge, stand two pieces of sculpture. One is a man known as Jonah who stands with a dolphin (yes, a dolphin) at his feet. In the old days the height of the river was measured by how far up his body the waters came. Sometimes it lapped his ankles, occasionally it reached his waist.

TURVEY
Bedfordshire

7 MILES (11 KM) WEST OF BEDFORD

The main road to Bedford crosses the River Great Ouse on an ancient stone-arched bridge to enter a village settled by the Beaker people as long ago as 1800BC. The Romans too were here, and the Saxons built a church on the site in about AD980. The medieval church which replaced it boasts some wonderful 13th-century iron scrollwork on the huge oak doors and an exquisite early 14th-century wall painting. The collection of funerary monuments is impressive, starting with Sir John Mordaunt, who died in 1506. The Mordaunts were lords of the manor from the 13th century until 1783, when the estate was bought by the Higgins family. Theirs is the large

Terraced cottages typical of this stone village

mausoleum in the churchyard. Turvey Abbey is a Jacobean house at the east end of the village, the former manor of the Higgins (subsequently Longuet-Higgins) family; it became an abbey in the true sense of the word only when bought by Benedictine sisters and monks in 1980. In Abbey Square are some pretty 17th-century estate-workers' cottages. It is to Charles Longuet-Higgins that the village owes much of its appearance today. He employed Gilbert Scott to restore the church in 1852, and it was he who built the school and most of the village's stone houses and cottages. Turvey House, with its highly decorated façade, was built in 1794.

The parish register for 1615 describes 'the greatest snow which ever fell uppon the Earth within man's memorye'. It lasted from January to May. Drifts covered walls and hedges and people went about 'without the sight of any earth, eyther uppon hilles or valleys'. On Kinder 'uppon May day in the morning, instead of fetching in flowers, the youthes brought in flakes of snow which lay above a foot deep uppon the moores and mountaynes'. In the Peaks of Derbyshire, nature still takes the leading role.

The village set in a limestone landscape that is patterned with the drystone walls built, stone by stone, about 200 years ago

YOULGREAVE
Derbyshire

4 MILES (6.5 KM) SOUTH OF BAKEWELL

Explore Derbyshire in the summer months and you are likely to come across the ancient art of well-dressing. It is not just wells that are dressed nowadays. In Youlgreave the public taps are adorned with these elaborate pictures made of flowers, mosses, seeds and cones, as well as its fountain. This is an attractive old lead-mining village high up in limestone Peakland. Its main street straggles along the hillside above the River Bradford, dominated by the big battlemented, pinnacled and gargoyled tower of the Norman church, one of the best in the area. Inside, it is all sturdy columns and capitals. The 13th-century font uniquely has two bowls, and there is a panel of similar date showing a Norman in a long robe. The excellent monuments include an effigy of Thomas Cokayne (*d*.1488) remarkable for its tiny size. The church was restored in 1870 by Norman Shaw and has stained-glass windows by Burne-Jones and Kempe. There are some good 18th-century stone houses near by, and to the west are Old Hall Farm (1630) and Old Hall (1650), both lovely hall houses. The area is rich in prehistory and 2 miles (3km) west of the village is Arbor Low, an Early Bronze Age stone circle, similar to but smaller than Stonehenge and Avebury. Its stones lie flat, in a circle about 250ft (76m) in diameter.

The writing shed at Laugharne, monument to a great Welsh poet

WALES AND THE WELSH MARCHES

The heights of Snowdon were hidden by the clouds but not from distance or dimness. The nearer hills, the other side of the valley, shewed a hard and beautifully detached and glimmering brim against the light, which was lifting there. All the length of the valley the skyline of the hills was flowing written all along the sky. A blue bloom, a sort of meal, seemed to have spread upon the distant south, enclosed by a basin of hills.

Gerard Manley Hopkins

*Black-and-white timbering
dating from Tudor days*

ABBOTS MORTON
Worcestershire

8 MILES (13 KM) NORTH OF EVESHAM

A perfect little black-and-white village, Abbots Morton is part of the rich legacy of the ancient Royal Forest of Ferndean that used to extend from Worcester and Bromsgrove to the Warwickshire border. The villages here originated as settlements in woodland clearings, though after felling in the Middle Ages for fuel for the local iron and salt industries and then in the 17th century for military supplies required by the Civil War, only vestiges of the forest remain. The forest was a well-known haunt and hiding place for the outlaws who regularly raided forest villages such as Abbots Morton, and the church was on these occasions a place of sanctuary for the villagers. It has stood since Norman times, at the western end of the village, surrounded by trees on slightly higher ground. It has a 14th-century tower, a low 15th-century doorway and inside is simplicity itself beneath the open timbers of its roof. Traces remain of paintwork on the gable over the chancel screen. It is also noted for its Jacobean altar rails. The village houses come in all shapes and sizes, some substantial, some tiny, in charming juxtapositions. The timbering of each and every one is a joy to study – and there is even a thatched letterbox.

ACTON BURNELL
Shropshire

7 MILES (11 KM) SOUTH OF SHREWSBURY

There is history in the name Acton Burnell: Acton was 'oak tun' (or 'settlement') to the Saxons, and Burnell is Robert Burnell. Robert Burnell was Bishop of Bath and Wells and Lord Chancellor of England at the time that Edward I was fighting the Marcher Lords. Between 1284 and 1293 Burnell built, on the eastern edge of the village, the fortified manor house whose roofless shell is now in the care of English Heritage. With warm red sandstone walls and towers, set off by the grey-green of an old cedar, the 'castle' has a somehow friendly aspect. Near by is the church that Burnell also built. There is much of interest: carving on the capitals, medieval floor tiles, the east window. Monuments include an excellent brass of Sir Nicholas Purnell (1382), an impressive alabaster of Sir Richard Lee whose family succeeded the Purnells, and memorials to the Smythes who owned the place from the 17th century and in the Georgian period built Acton Burnell Hall. Also near by are the remains of a large barn, probably the site of a meeting of a parliament held in the village when Edward I visited Bishop Burnell in 1283. Four roads meet in the village – all have pretty houses, some half-timbered black-and-white and some Georgian brick.

*Into my heart an air that kills
From yon far country blows
What are those blue
    remembered hills,
What spires, what farms are
    those?*

*This is the land of lost content,
I see it shining plain,
The happy highways where I
    went
And cannot come again.*

A E Housman, 'The Welsh Marches'

The village is a blend of Tudor black-and-white and Georgian brick – this Georgian house has been given a 'Tudor' façade

BEDDGELERT
Gwynedd

7 MILES (11 KM) NORTH OF PORTHMADOG

*O'erturned his infant's bed he
found
With bloodstained covert rent
And all around, the walls and
ground
With recent blood besprent…
'Hell hound! my child's by
thee devoured'
The frantic father cry'd
And to the hilt his vengeful
sword
He plung'd in Gelert's side…*

Variants of the Gelert legend
are early and widespread. It
is the stuff of balladeers
like 19th-century William
Spencer, above.

*A particularly attractive
group of shops, inns and
cottages around the two-
arched bridge over the
Afon Glaslyn*

*I*n the heart of Snowdonia's ravishing scenery, Beddgelert is a truly delightful mountain village, built of hunky slate-stone. Many of its houses were built in the 19th century as guesthouses and hotels for Victorian visitors to the area. One of the oldest monasteries in Wales once stood in the nearby meadows, succeeded by a 12th-century Augustinian priory dedicated to a St Kelert who gave the village its original name. The church is all that remains, and much of that is 19th-century, but it has some surprisingly sophisticated 13th-century arcading and window lancets. The Royal Goat Inn is connected with the famous legend of Prince Llywelyn's dog Gelert, left by his master to guard his infant son. When Llywelyn returned to find the cot upturned and Gelert covered in blood, he assumed the dog had killed the child and shot him instantly. Too late, he found his son alive and well beside the body of a wolf from whose jaws poor Gelert had saved him. A good story, and more likely to attract trade to the village than St Kelert, or so it seems the Goat's first innkeeper in 1798 felt. He built Gelert a convincing grave ('bedd') near the church, thereby burying the name of the saint and giving lasting fame to 'Beddgelert'.

A cottage whose blend of thatch, stone and brick typifies the village as a whole

BREDON
Worcestershire

3 MILES (5 KM) NORTH-EAST OF TEWKESBURY

*B*redon is a lovely old place that has grown up over the ages. The 20th century too has made its contribution, with extensive modern housing on one side and the M5 streaking across the other, but at its heart it remains as charming as ever and has some exceptional treasures. The houses in the older part are a harmonious mixture of timber frame, red brick and Cotswold stone (Bredon Hill being an outlier of the Cotswolds), with some thatch. Unusually for this area, a spire beckons us to the magnificent church. It has several Norman and medieval features, notably three 12th-century doorways and some armorial, Worcestershire tiles. It also houses a splendid monument to Sir Charles Reed, who in 1696 endowed the pretty almshouses at the other end of Church Street. Near the church is the old rectory, a distinguished, although recently altered, building. Little figures of Cromwell and Charles I ride along the roof; if they meet, 'tis said, the world will end. The Old Mansion is a beauty in 17th-century red brick with mullioned windows. The 18th-century manor house too is good, but the real jewel is its medieval tithe barn. All tithe barns are big, but this is one of the largest and finest in Britain, with a massive stone-tiled roof. An outside staircase leads to a room over one of its doorways.

In summertime on Bredon
The bells they sound so clear;
Round both the shires they ring
*   them*
In steeples far and near,
A happy noise to hear.

Here of a Sunday morning
My love and I would lie,
And see the coloured counties,
And hear the larks so high
About us in the sky.

A E Housman, 'Summertime on Bredon'

CAREW
Pembrokeshire

3 MILES (5 KM) EAST OF PEMBROKE

*A*t high tide the Carew River mirrors the roofless ruin of Carew Castle in the waters of a creek of Milford Haven. At low tide the turrets seem to emerge from the mudflats, for it is set low, strategically guarding the river approach. The castle was first built when the land was given to the Norman Gerald de Windsor by the Prince of Deheubarth in 1095, as part of his daughter Nesta's dowry. Nesta, a woman of great beauty, was abducted from the castle by Owain ap Cadwgan. One hopes she did not go too reluctantly, for she was with Owain long enough to bear him at least two children before Gerald reclaimed her. The great drum towers date to the 13th century, the great hall was added in the 15th century by Sir Rhys ap Thomas, and the north side was reconstructed in domestic vein by Sir John Perrot, an illegitimate son of Henry VIII. Sir Rhys

Below: the romantic ruin of Carew Castle, set on an inlet of Milford Haven. Opposite: Carew's restored 16th-century French Tidal Mill

ap Thomas, it is believed, gave hospitality to Henry Tudor when he landed at Pembroke on his return from exile in France on 7 August 1485. He then fought at Henry's side at Bosworth, and some say it was he who killed Richard III. Safely on the throne, Henry rewarded Rhys by making him a Knight of the Garter and in celebration Rhys held a five-day tournament here, generally agreed to be the greatest ever staged in Wales.

To the west of the castle is the French Tidal Mill, so called because the stones used to build it in the 16th century came from France. It is one of only three restored tidal mills in Britain and is open to the public. In the main street near the castle is Carew Cross, one of the most important Celtic crosses in Wales. It

dates from around 1033, is over 13ft (4m) high and commemorates an early ruler of this area, Maredudd ap Edwin. The cross is intricately carved and its interlacing patterns are exceptionally well preserved. As if by contrast, an 1852 Wesleyan chapel stands close by. The Carew Arms adjoins it. Just a spit away across the fields from the old stone cottages and the new housing estate is the village church, actually in Carew Cheriton. This too is special. It dates from the 14th century and has a spacious, medieval feel to it. The effigies include one believed to be that of Sir Nicholas Carew who owned the castle in Edward I's day. In the churchyard is a little chantry chapel, unusually detached from the church and a rare survival.

Rhys ap Thomas, owner of Carew Castle in 1485, came from a strongly Lancastrian family. Only a few years before he sheltered the future Henry VII on his return from exile, however, he had for a while been a supporter of Richard III and had declared that Henry would enter Wales only over his body. In order to square his conscience about this when Henry arrived in Pembroke, it is said, he hid under a bridge near Dale so that Henry did indeed ride into Wales over his body.

A slate-stone terrace of one-time slate-miners' cottages

DINAS MAWDDWY
Gwynedd

8 MILES (13 KM) SOUTH OF DOLGELLAU

Traditionally famous for 'false men, blue earth and ceaseless rain', Dinas is in fact a delightful village set among folding hills where the Cerist meets the Dovey to swell the limpid waters so popular with fishermen. To say the rain is ceaseless is perhaps to exaggerate just a little, but the blue earth can rightly be associated with the lead mining that was the traditional industry of the village before slate quarrying took over. As for the false men, the belief has probably much to do with the notorious Red Robbers of Mawddwy, 80 of whom were finally caught and executed in 1555 after years of terrorising all and sundry. Today the locals are friendly, welcoming visitors to its hostelries, The Red Lion and The Buckley Arms. The Red Lion is the oldest building in the village, supposedly frequented by Henry I's illegitimate son Robert while visiting the infamously beautiful Nesta, who had been kidnapped from Carew Castle by Owain ap Cadwgan and reputedly lived in one of the shops in the main street. In the 19th century a Manchester businessman, Edmund Buckley, tried to save Dinas's fortunes as a bustling market centre from decline by building a railway. Neither markets nor railway survive, but Buckley's name lives on and the old station is now a café for visitors to the cloth-mill.

DOLWYDDELAN
Conwy

5 MILES (8 KM) SOUTH-WEST OF BETWYS-Y-COED

Mountains are all around, but Dolwyddelan itself is set in an open valley, with houses of dark slate set back from the waters of the Lledr. The main street of this old slate-quarrying village is dominated by a large, double-doored Victorian Methodist chapel, while further along are another chapel and the Church of St Gwyddelan, a Celtic saint who founded a church here in the 6th century. The present church, a little gem with slate floor and whitened walls, was built early in the 16th century by Meredydd ap Ieuan, Prince of Powis, to whom there is (unusually for Wales) a fine brass. The 7th-century bell may be that which Gwyddelan brought with him from Ireland, and there is a good 15th-century rood screen, perhaps from an earlier church. On a rocky knoll to the west of the village is the tower of Dolwyddelan Castle. The castle was built late in the 12th century, traditionally the birthplace of Llywelyn the Great (though this is unsubstantiated). It was a basic castle, with one wall around a courtyard, and it remained in Welsh hands only until 1283 when Edward I added it to the list of fortresses with which he was encircling the Welsh. Behind it looms the peak of Moel Siabod, a challenge for mountaineers.

The mountains of Snowdonia are a backdrop to another slate-stone village

EARDISLAND
Herefordshire

5 MILES (8 KM) WEST OF LEOMINSTER

A picture postcard village of black-and-white timbering and mellow stone, Eardisland is at its most scenic around the old stone bridges across the River Arrow and its mill race. The mill itself has gone but the old mill house stands astride the stream, a Georgian stone building as lovely as any mill house can be. The timber-framed cottage opposite was built as the school in 1652 and still has the old village whipping post and manacles at its northern end. The timber-framed manor house dates from the 17th century with a brick extension of the Queen Anne period. In its garden is a beautiful old, tall dovecote, red-brick and gabled. This whole grouping is set off by green lawns beside the river. North of the river is the village's most striking building, a very old, sprawling house with a delectably saggy sandstone-tiled roof. It was built in about 1300 as a yeoman's hall house and had wings added in the 16th and the 17th centuries (this one incorporating a dovecote). The church is basically Norman but heavily restored inside. Look over the north wall of the churchyard for a view of the huge old moated castle mound around which the village first grew up in Norman days.

The 17th-century manor house with its green lawns

ELMLEY CASTLE
Worcestershire

4 MILES (6.5 KM) SOUTH-WEST OF EVESHAM

*The main street, showing
The Queen Elizabeth Inn*

The castle no longer exists. It was built in the 11th century, ruined by 1300, refortified in the 14th century and finally ruined again during the 16th century. The village, however, has survived the centuries to be, so it has been claimed, one of the most beautiful in the country. Just beneath the north-east slope of Bredon Hill, Elmley Castle is altogether charming, but most memorable particularly for its wide main street with its stream and predominantly black-and-white half-timbered houses. Infill and new housing are never disagreeable. The street runs from the 15th-century cross at the northern end to the church at the top, near The Queen Elizabeth Inn, a pretty Tudor establishment which recalls Elizabeth I's visit to the Savage family in the castle in 1575. The square-towered, stone-built 11th-century church is richly rewarding. Look first for the sundials in the churchyard and then, inside, for the dragons on the medieval base of the font. Two of the monuments are special: the beautifully carved alabaster memorial to the Savage family and the marvellous monument to the 1st Earl of Coventry and his second wife, placed here and not in the family church at Croome, it is said, because the 2nd Earl disapproved of his stepmother's 'mean' ancestry.

The two outstanding monuments in the church make an interesting lesson in the development of sculpture during the 17th century: the earlier Savage family group a work of art very much in medieval style – recumbent figures, heraldry, the children kneeling along the side; then, in contrast, the 1699 black and white marble concoction by William Stanton, quite different but of its day equally splendid – reclining figure, standing angels, columns and pediments.

In spring the churchyard and the lanes around it are full of daffodils, but the church is lovely at any season

KILPECK
Herefordshire

8 MILES (13 KM) SOUTH-WEST OF HEREFORD

The origins of the Hereford School of carving are interesting and debatable. Certainly, little of the decoration of Kilpeck can be . attributed to Normandy. The chancel carvings are similar to some in Compostela, in Spain, and it is known that one Oliver de Merlimont, who founded nearby Shobdon Church a few years before Kilpeck was built, travelled to Compostela. Whatever the answer, undoubtedly some credit must go to the inspiration of the local craftsmen as well. Other examples of the flowering of the Hereford School may be found at nearby Brinsop and Stretton Sugwas.

Kilpeck is a quiet place in the lanes of Herefordshire, a mix of stone and half-timbered houses. There is a 15th-century manor house and some crumbling masonry on a castle mound, but it is the church that is important – important and exquisite. It is tiny and just about entirely Norman, of the mid-12th century. It also has some of the most stunning Romanesque carving in Britain, the work of the famous Hereford School of carving. The south doorway makes a good start. Dragons, birds and a flying angel are ranged around the arch, on the jambs are two warriors in peaked caps and baggy trousers and one dragon that swallows another's tail – all in a tangle of foliage. Around the outside of the building are 80 or so carved corbels, deliciously fanciful and uninhibited. A few are gone, removed by modest Victorians (there is one female erotic, or fertility, figure that they missed, however). The red sandstone used was clearly well-chosen, for the carvings have survived the 800 years amazingly well. Inside, the chancel arch is also decoratively carved, with elongated apostles. There is a primitive, perhaps Saxon, stoup – a pot belly clasped by a pair of hands – and a huge Norman font. And, in the graveyard, do not miss some magnificently decorative late-Georgian tombstones.

LAUGHARNE
Carmarthenshire

4 MILES (6.5 KM) SOUTH OF ST CLEARS

Situated on the western shores of the estuary of the River Taf, this is a village with a long history, but it is for its associations with Dylan Thomas that it is chiefly known. Dylan Thomas lived here with his wife Caitlin in The Boathouse, a 'sea-shaken house on a breakneck of rocks' that is now a museum. It was in the old blue-painted garage overlooking his 'heron priested shore' that he wrote *Under Milk Wood*, the radio play that so evocatively describes a day in an imaginary Welsh village. He died in America, in an alcoholic coma, in 1953 but is buried in the churchyard here. The street that leads down from the church into the centre is lined with elegant three-storey Georgian houses, many colour-washed, while the houses and cottages of the streets near the square (The Grist) are of mellow, reddish stone with slate roofs. Brown's Hotel was a favourite haunt of the poet. Near the foreshore is the ruined castle (in the care of Cadw Welsh Historic Monuments). In its early days it was repeatedly wrecked by the Welsh and recaptured by the Normans. In Tudor times Henry VIII's illegitimate son Sir John Perrot reconstructed it as a mansion, but it was subsequently attacked again by Cromwell's men, leaving the romantic ruin we see today, the subject of one of Turner's paintings.

Looking along the main street towards the clock tower and belfry of the town hall, built in 1746

Laugharne was given its charter in 1307 and has to this day retained its status as a borough. Twice a year the Corporation elects its leader, the Portreeve. The Portreeve, wearing a chain of gold cockle shells as a reflection of a one-time source of wealth, is installed with his attendants at a formal breakfast. At its annual banquet the Corporation of Laugharne toasts its founder, Sir Guy de Brian.

NEW RADNOR
Powys

New Radnor was 'new' in 1064. Harold Godwineson, Earl of Wessex, founded an English stronghold here (or so it is believed), having previously destroyed Old Radnor. Two years later, in January 1066, he became King Harold II and in October was killed at the battle of Hastings. New Radnor was given to the Norman baron, Philip de Braose.

New Radnor is situated at the head of a short valley leading from England into Wales, between the mountains of Radnor Forest to the north-west and the hill called Smatcher to the south, and in this commanding position the Normans built a motte and bailey. In 1188 the village was the starting point of Archbishop Baldwin's tour through Wales with Gerald of Wales, drumming up support for the Third Crusade. In the middle of the 13th century the Normans built a new castle on the same site. The town they built below the castle was laid out as

A view of the village showing the Victorian church, the castle mound and the monument

a grid pattern enclosed by a rectangular rampart, in a similar plan to that they used in Winchelsea (see page 69). From the old castle mound (all that is left of the castle) both the street pattern and the line of the walls can clearly be seen. The Welsh and the Normans spent the next 300 years destroying and rebuilding the place, until finally it fell for the last time to Cromwell in 1644.

The town used to be a borough and the county town of Radnorshire, but as other towns grew in importance, New Radnor went into decline. Reminders of its earlier status exist in Broad Street, in the old town hall which has a lock-up behind, and the Eagle Hotel which stands on the site of the old prison. There is something of an eye-opener at the bottom of Broad Street: the Cornewall Lewis Monument is an exuberantly over-the-top-Victorian memorial by John Gibbs, strongly reminiscent of Prince Albert's in London. George Cornewall Lewis was New Radnor's MP from 1855 to 1863 and Palmerston's Chancellor of the Exchequer, Home Secretary and War Minister. Water Street leads back up from the monument towards the castle mound. It is aptly named, for a stream runs along its length and the houses are reached by little bridges. At the top end is a timber-framed farm. In the third main street, Rectory Lane, is the old Zion chapel and a charming, tiny graveyard. Back up under the castle mound is the village church, built in Gothic style in the 1840s on the site of a medieval one that was demolished to make way for it.

The Cornewall Lewis memorial, perhaps the grandest in Wales

Metely well walled…
There is an old church standing now as a chapel by the castle…The building of the town is some part metely good, in most part but rude, many houses being thatched. The castle is in ruin…The town was defaced in Henry IV days by Owain Glyndwr.
From a 16th-century description of New Radnor by John Leland

PEMBRIDGE
Herefordshire

6 MILES (9.5 KM) WEST OF LEOMINSTER

*T*his is Herefordshire cattle country, and the market hall in the square is evidence of Pembridge's days as a market centre. It dates from early in the 16th century, its stone-tiled roof supported on oak columns. On its east side are two stones which are thought to be 'nails' on which bargains were struck, as in the phrase 'paying on the nail'. Also in the square are the New Inn, some 200 years older (and, they say, haunted), some half-timbered buildings of varying dates, and a flight of steps that leads uphill to the churchyard. The large 14th-century church is especially remarkable for its detached belfry.

Pembridge has one of the best collections of black-and-white houses in the county

There are several in Herefordshire, but this is the finest example, a reflection of Pembridge's status as a borough in medieval days. During Border skirmishes it would have served as a stronghold, with a commanding view out over the Welsh Marches. The compact village is a feast of black-and-white, with numerous early cruck houses and dozens of timber-framed and jettied buildings with all sorts of detail to delight the eye. Many have stone-tiled roofs. In Bridge Street, which leads down to the River Arrow, Duppa's almshouses date from 1661. Another set of almshouses, Trafford's, in East Street, dates from 1686.

Founding Father
Clough Williams-Ellis was born in 1883 and became a keen conservationist and innovative designer. His work as an architect includes post-World War II New Towns such as Stevenage. In Portmeirion he achieved his ambition of proving that a site can be developed without spoiling it, creating his model resort village 'free from advertisements and careless building'. He was knighted for services to architecture and the environment in 1971, six years before he died.

PORTMEIRION
Gwynedd

2 MILES (3 KM) SOUTH-EAST OF PORTHMADOG

Created before and after World War II, the buildings of Portmeirion were designated in 1971 as being of particular historical and architectural interest

Portmeirion is a fairy-tale extravaganza, a masterpiece of a folly, the Italianate concoction of Sir Clough Williams-Ellis set on a craggy, wooded peninsula above the sands of a river estuary in the wilds of North Wales. Enchanted as a young man by Italy and in particular by the sunny fishing village of Portofino, this distinguished Welsh architect determined to build something at home that captured its atmosphere. He spent some years searching for a suitable site before this estate came to his notice in 1925. He cleared the wilderness that had grown up around the few buildings already there, and started to build the fanciful collection of romantic buildings that make up this magic place. Towers and turrets, porticoes and balconies, spires and domes jostle with fountains and pools and statues in a vista of pastel pink and yellow walls, green lawns and colourfully exotic shrubs. There is a triumphal arch, a domed Pantheon, an elegant campanile. Some of the buildings were entirely Sir Clough's invention, some are pieces rescued from all over the place and put into his 'home for fallen buildings', like the magnificent plastered ceiling of the town hall retrieved from a demolished mansion in Flintshire. From the start visitors have been charged to enter this triumphantly romantic and colourful dream village.

Stone-built cottages of a village that is dominated by its romantic valley ruins

---

TALLEY
Carmarthenshire

7 MILES (11 KM) NORTH OF LLANDEILO

The great medieval Welsh poet Dafydd ap Gwilym is reputed to be buried here. A humourist and something of a ladies' man, he is remembered especially for his love poetry.

Beauty, come to the hillside,
Our bed be high on the hill,
Four ages under the fresh
* birches,*
Valanced with brilliant ferns,
A coverlet, against beating
* rain,*
Of trees that check the shower.
(Translated by Gwyn Williams)

Talyllychau, of which 'Talley' is a corruption, means 'head of the lakes', and it was on the southern shores of the upper of Talley's two glacial lakes that in 1120 Rhys ap Gruffydd founded an abbey for the Premonstratensian order. The villagers of Talley today still enjoy the peace and solitude that the 12th-century monks found here, their white-walled and colour-washed houses clustering round the silent abbey ruins beneath the wooded slopes of Mynydd Cynros. Talley was the only foundation of White Canons in Wales. It suffered heavy damage in Owain Glyndwr's uprising and by the time of the dissolution only eight monks

remained here. The abbey was pillaged for building stone and all that remains are two walls of the church's central tower, supported on high pointed arches. The ruins are beautiful, and are in the care of Cadw, Welsh Historic Monuments. An 18th-century church stands near by, built for the village when the church that was the abbey church fell into disrepair. It is quietly simple, with bellcote, flagged floor, clear-glazed windows and old box pews set out in Welsh chapel style. Its walled graveyard runs down to the lake-shore. A Georgian farmhouse stands among trees in one corner, and the pub stands a little away from the heart of the village.

WEOBLEY
Herefordshire

9 MILES (14.5 KM) SOUTH-WEST OF LEOMINSTER

For lovers of black and white, Weobley is an incomparable treasure-house. In the Middle Ages the manufacture of ale and gloves brought prosperity and borough status. Indeed, so important did the place become that until the Reform Bill of 1832 it was a borough that returned two MPs. The spire of the church proclaims this medieval wealth from afar. It is 14th-century, a splendid thing, pinnacled and buttressed, and is a feature rarely found in the churches of the Marches. It is an interesting church with some Norman work and, by way of contrast, a splendid late 17th-century monument to Colonel Birch, who played a leading role in the Restoration. The rest of the village, with the exception of a few Georgian frontages, is overwhelmingly black-and-white. Some of the buildings date back to the 1300s, others are 15th-, 16th- or 17th-century. A number were demolished in the 19th century and earlier this century a fire in the main street destroyed yet more. In this area, the site of the old market place, there is now a walled garden. Only by exploring the streets that lead off it can justice be done to the craftsmanship of the cruck frames, cross braces, angle posts and carved details that are the making of these buildings.

Weobley has several inns of note. The Unicorn is the work of John Abel (1577–1674), a great master builder and, it seems, the leading Herefordshire craftsman of his time. He also built the town hall which was destroyed in about 1860, as well as other buildings that have also now gone. The finest remaining example of his work in Herefordshire is probably in Leominster, the old market hall at the top of Broad Street.

The Red Lion and the building behind it are some of the village's finest

The hanging sign which adorns Haworth's literary shrine

NORTH COUNTRY

Then afterward we found a long green dale
Walled up to heaven with all its scattered farms,
And lean fields parcelled out with dun stone walls
And ragged clouds piled on the moor's faint arms.

Wilfrid Rowland Childe,
'Haworth in May'

The Lord Crewe Arms was at one time the home of General Tom Forster, who was arrested for involvement in the Jacobite rising in 1715. He escaped and was hidden by his sister, Dorothy, in a priest's hole behind a fireplace in the house. Dorothy is said to appear now and then as a ghost, asking for a message to be taken to her brother who fled to France.

BLANCHLAND
Northumberland

9 MILES (14.5 KM) SOUTH OF HEXHAM

*B*lanchland is hidden at the foot of wooded slopes deep in the valley of the River Derwent, like a well-kept secret. So well-kept that Scots on a Border raid in 1327 failed to find it and moved off. The monks of Blanchland Abbey rang a peal of bells in thanksgiving, but of course the Scots heard it, returned and sacked the place. A Premonstratensian order of monks founded the abbey in 1165 and stayed until the dissolution, when the place fell into disrepair. In 1752 the estate came into the hands of the trustees of Lord Crewe and they began repairs and restoration, keeping the collegiate layout of the village. Parts of the 13th-century abbey church

survive as the parish church, and the remains of the cloisters may be seen in the garden of the Lord Crewe Arms, a building which incorporates part of the monks' refectory and guesthouse. The old, dark stone gatehouse, in which there is now a shop, makes an intriguing, cobbled entrance to the village square. The hard-surfaced 'square' is in fact L-shaped, and neatly ranged round it are the greyish sandstone cottages that were built to house workers in the lead-mining industry that started up locally in the mid-18th century. Blanchland is thus an early and delightful planned industrial village, perfect in setting and in construction.

The stone bridge over the Derwent, leading into the village

BOLTON BY BOWLAND
Lancashire

6 MILES (9.5 KM) NORTH-EAST OF CLITHEROE

The extraordinary monument to the Pudsay family

The Kirk Beck, a tributary of the River Ribble, flows through this secluded stone village, above the lower of its two greens. Here stand a pair of stocks and the stump of a 13th-century market cross, overlooked by the Coach and Horses Inn. Stocks House is a substantial house dating from 1835. The more modest stone cottages are mostly whitewashed, one having an outside staircase leading directly to the first floor workshop, now a gunsmith. The upper, and larger, green, shaded by trees, is faced by the 19th-century church school and the former courthouse where dwelling rights for the Forest of Bowland used to be decided. All around are more stone cottages. The church repays close scrutiny. On the doorpost are marks made by bowmen sharpening their arrows – the name of this area, Bowland, is said to come from the longbows made from local yews. Look out, too, for the lepers' squint and, on the font cover, the mouse signature of carver Robert Thompson. More immediately noticeable is the monument on which are carved the figures of Sir Ralph Pudsay, his three wives and their 25 children. The Pudsays were lords of the manor from 1349 to 1771, and the church was rebuilt by Sir Ralph during 1464, the same year that he sheltered Lancastrian Henry VI from his Yorkist foes.

*The main street, seen from
the western end*

BOWES
Durham

5 MILES (8 KM) SOUTH-WEST OF BARNARD CASTLE

*At Bowes begins the great
grazing country for children. It
is the cheapest part of
England, and schools for boys
have long been established
here, to which tradesmen and
even some parents of higher
order who think money better
than learning, send their
children from all the great
towns...*
Robert Southey, *Letters from
England* (1807)

An old Roman road (the A66) strides across wild moorland landscape and passes along the village street. Solid grey stone houses line the route that was guarded first by a Roman fort and later by Bowes Castle. The Normans built the castle around 1180, using stone from the settlement the Romans had called *Lavatrae*. The hefty, square chunk of its keep (the only stone building in castle) still stands, passages and staircases winding within its 12ft-(2.6m) thick walls. Near by is the church, also built of stone from the Roman fort, within the bounds of which it stands. It has a beautiful medieval carved stone crucifixion outside the south porch and, within, a Roman dedication slab of about AD204 and two ancient fonts. In the grave-yard is the tombstone of 19-year-old George Ashton Taylor. It was this that so moved Charles Dickens and gave him inspiration for the character of Smike in *Nicholas Nickleby*. While staying at the Ancient Unicorn Inn Dickens saw stagecoaches delivering boys destined for one of the boarding schools in the area. One of them, a building set back from the road and now a private house, is said to be the original of Dotheboys Hall, run by Dickens's Wackford Squeers – William Shaw in real life. Members of the Shaw family are also buried in the church.

CARTMEL
Cumbria

13 MILES (21 KM) SOUTH-WEST OF KENDAL

Cartmel is an ancient and lovely place, sited in the middle of a peninsula that juts out on to the sands of Morecambe Bay. The great priory pervades its every corner. The Church of St Mary and St Michael dates from the founding of the Augustinian priory by William Marshall, later Earl of Pembroke, at the end of the 12th century and, unusually, survived the dissolution intact, remaining in use as the parish church. Inside are massive columns, a vast east window and some wonderful carving (do not miss the exquisite misericords). Externally, the diagonally set tower dwarfs the houses of the village at its feet. The only other remnant of the priory complex is its gatehouse in the small cobbled square. The one large room over the archway was used as a lock-up and then in the 17th and 18th centuries as a school, and it is now in the care of the National Trust. Cottages and shops of stone or traditional roughcast, sometimes painted, make attractive groupings round the square and in the streets that lead off it. Many of the houses were constructed using stone from the demolished priory buildings. One street runs down to the little River Eea, another out past the racecourse where meetings are held on bank holiday weekends.

The Norman gatehouse of the old priory

Treacherous Sands
Before the railway arrived, travellers to Lancaster and Ulverston would often risk the shortcut 'over the sands' routes that are indicated on a milestone in the village. Many lost their lives on these dangerous sands, and now lie buried in the churchyard.

STERNE WAS THE MAN WHO WITH GIGANTIC STRIDE
MOW'D DOWN LUXURIANT FOLLIES FAR AND WIDE
(Inscription on Laurence Sterne's tombstone, to be seen in the churchyard)

COXWOLD
North Yorkshire

8 MILES (13 KM) SOUTH-EAST OF THIRSK

There is something more than the name that is reminiscent of the Cotswolds here. Set at the end of the Howardian Hills, the village's limestone houses share that same, warm, honey colouring. The main street is steep and wide, with broad cobbled paving, grassy banks and trees between its mellow houses. The almshouses were built in 1662 by Mary, daughter of Oliver Cromwell and wife of Thomas Earl of Fauconberg, commemorated by the Fauconberg Arms further up the hill. Mary is supposed to have buried her father's headless body in nearby Newburgh Priory in a brick vault which has never been opened. At the top of the hill are two more distinguished 17th-century buildings: Old Hall, once a grammar school, and Colville Hall, behind the church. From the octagonal-towered church there are good views eastwards over the attractive village roofscape. It was here that Laurence Sterne was parson for eight years, from 1760 until his death. He lived in a house near the church, naming it Shandy Hall, 'shandy' being a local word for eccentric. Eccentricity is a quality Sterne himself could claim, of course. It was here that he wrote Volumes 3-9 of that famous medley *Tristram Shandy*, and also *A Sentimental Journey through France and Italy...* The house is open to the public, and stuffed with memorabilia.

Laurence Sterne's Shandy Hall, mellow brick in an otherwise golden limestone village

The upper storeys of the tall houses used to have balconies on which the 'terrible knitters of Dent', as they became known, would knit up the local wool into stockings, gloves and caps. Sometimes these assiduous folk used sheaths, often beautifully decorated, to hold one needle, tucking them into a belt so that one hand was left free to knead the dough or smoke a pipe.

DENT
Cumbria

6 MILES (9.5 KM) SOUTH-WEST OF SEDBERGH

Cottage doors open directly on to the cobbled streets

The tightly packed streets of sturdy stone cottages make a striking contrast with the bleak fell landscape all around the village. Dent just sits there quietly and unspoilt, the only real community in Dentdale. Courts and alleyways lead off its winding cobbled streets; some of the terraced houses are whitewashed, some are tall and narrow, heavy stone-tiled roofs protecting them from the vagaries of the weather. In the church – a simple Dales church that has grown from Norman origins – are the pews of the 24 Dentdale 'statesmen', or owner-farmers, who in 1429 constituted a form of local government. It was the Vikings who in the 9th and 10th centuries created this owner-farmer system of narrow, parallel strips of farmland, each with its spring and share of good valley bottom pasture and rough upland. Also in the church is a memorial to Professor Adam Sedgwick, the distinguished geologist who was born here, son of the parson, in 1785. As a small boy he attended the grammar school, a little building in the churchyard. In the main street a slab of Shap granite commemorates this great local benefactor. In Sedgwick's day Dent was a community of 2000 people, entirely self-sufficient, practising many trades that included marble quarrying, coal mining, horse breeding and knitting. Most have gone.

Typical gritstone buildings, the dark stone picked out with light mortar

DOBCROSS
Greater Manchester

4 MILES (6.5 KM) EAST OF OLDHAM

Dobcross is a village of enormous interest for the social historian and industrial archaeologist. It grew up in the 18th century at the junction of two packhorse routes in the Pennine foothills, and until about 1850 was the commercial and social heart of the Saddleworth weaving district. It has survived intact, its austere, dark gritstone buildings a perfect reflection of developments in the woollen trade at the time. An expansion in the domestic weaving industry locally led to the building of cottages with purpose-built rooms for the workers' looms, usually on the second floor, and there are a number of these houses in Dobcross, clearly distinguished by

the long rows of stone-mullioned windows that provided the necessary light. The tall, terraced weavers' cottages and larger clothiers' and merchants' houses line the narrow streets and stand haphazardly in the cobbled square at the top of the village. The square has changed little in 200 years. Around it can also be seen a range of warehouses, a row of shops dated 1789, the 18th-century Swan Inn and the former Saddleworth Bank building of 1813. Dobcross was the birthplace of the giant textile machinery business, Platt Brothers. It was on prosperity such as theirs that the village church was built in 1787, in the unpretentious style of a preaching house.

ELSDON
Northumberland

21 MILES (34 KM) NORTH OF HEXHAM

At first glance Elsdon may look like a place whose story can only be a peaceful one. Old stone farmworkers' cottages, a pub, an ancient church, a 7 acre (2.8ha) village green, rolling hills all around. But probe a little and some of history's bloodier moments come to light, for Elsdon was once the 'capital' of Redesdale, a lawless, wild and windy place and the setting for grisly Border skirmishes between Scots and English in the Middle Ages. St Cuthbert's Church stands among trees in the upper half of the green, mostly 14th-century, clear-glazed and beautifully bare. During restoration work a mass grave was uncovered, believed to hold bodies from the Battle of Otterburn in 1388. Not far from the church, in a commanding position, is the former parsonage, Elsdon Tower, which also dates from the 14th century. This is one of the most important pele towers, or fortified houses, in the county and has defensive walls up to 8ft (2.5m) thick. The village houses, mostly 18th-century, some modern, surround the green that saw annual fairs and weekly markets from the 13th century on, but was also a stockade to keep cattle safe from raids. The stone-walled circular pound survives, and an oak tree marks the spot where bear baiting and cock fighting once entertained the villagers.

Just behind the village, beside the road, are the Mote Hills, the well-preserved, grass-covered earthworks of a Norman motte and bailey which was built by the D'Umphraville family in about 1080.

The village green, with the Coronation Oak and the church

GAWSWORTH
Cheshire

4 MILES (6.5 KM) SOUTH-WEST OF MACCLESFIELD

Below: Elizabethan Gawsworth Old Hall, now open to the public. Above: Fitton family monuments in the church

Ornamental pools make a beautiful and unusual setting for this lovely village and its exceptional collection of buildings – two halls, two rectories and a good church. Most notable of all these is Gawsworth Old Hall, a magnificent half-timbered building with some interesting historical connections. The 'fighting' Fittons had been lords of the manor here from 1316 and it was they who built the Old Hall in the 16th century. It has a three-decker bay window looking on to the gardens, a panel on the north front carved and signed by Richard Rany in 1570, and some splendid internal timbering. In the park is a tilting ground, 200yds (183m) long and over 60yds (55m) wide, now believed to be a rare example of an Elizabethan pleasure ground. One of the most famous Fittons was Mary, who became maid of honour to Elizabeth I in about 1595 but soon disgraced herself by having an affair with William Herbert, later Earl of Pembroke. Twice married and twice widowed, she is thought by some to be the mysterious 'dark lady' of Shakespeare's sonnets. She is indeed represented as dark in colouring on the painted family monument in the church. Another character associated with the Old Hall is one Samuel Johnson, who was England's last professional court jester. He was also a playwright, hitting the London limelight briefly with an opera called *Hurlothrumbo*. Success went to his head and he wrote three more plays. All flopped and he returned to Gawsworth, dying in 1773 at the ripe age of 82 and being buried at his request in nearby Maggoty Johnson's Wood (National Trust).

The New Hall near by, also looking on to the ponds, was started in 1707 for Lord Mohun who in 1712 famously entered into a duel against the Duke of Hamilton, during which both died. The duel is described in Thackeray's *Henry Esmond*. The Old Rectory is another black-and-white building, dating from 1470. Its central hall has finely carved timbering to its open roof. The present rectory was built in 1707 as a school. The church stands close to it among yew trees, a 15th-century building on Norman foundations with pinnacles and battlements, gargoyles and heraldic shields. Inside, the nave has a good painted roof and a 400-year-old font, while in the chancel are the Fitton family monuments. Sir Edward Fitton and his wife married when they were 12, and had 15 children, one of them being the father of dark Mary.

*Dove Cottage, favourite home
of the Wordsworths*

GRASMERE
Cumbria

9 MILES (14.5 KM) NORTH-WEST OF WINDERMERE

*Dove Cottage, favourite home
of the Wordsworths*

Purplish grey-green houses tucked into the wooded lower slopes of Lakeland's grassy hills – in William Wordsworth's words, 'the loveliest spot that man hath ever found'. Grasmere would surely find a place in every guidebook on its own merits, but it is for its associations with Wordsworth and his family that it is best known. In 1799 William and his sister Dorothy moved into Dove Cottage and it was here that he wrote poems such as 'Intimations of Immortality', 'Ode to Duty', 'The Brothers' and *The Prelude*. In 1802 Wordsworth married Mary Hutchinson and brought her to live here too. They loved the place, entertaining numerous friends, including Scott and Coleridge, and enjoying excursions into the hills and on the lake. But with a growing family they moved to Allan Bank, which Wordsworth never liked, and then to the parsonage in 1811, finally leaving Grasmere for Rydal in 1813. After the Wordsworth family moved out, Dove Cottage became the home of Thomas de Quincey, author of *The Confessions of an English Opium Eater*. It has now been restored and guided tours may be taken. Near by is the Wordsworth Museum which houses memorabilia of the Wordsworth family and the friends who visited them here.

Dove Cottage, a little way out from the village centre, is whitewashed but most of Grasmere's buildings are of the distinctive bluish-green local slate. Old cottages and shops, Victorian villas and guesthouses, galleries and hotels line the twisty main street. To the east the River Rothay winds down the back of the village to Grasmere Lake, passing St Oswald's Church on its way. The church is faced with pebbledash outside but parts date from the 14th century at least. It was described by Wordsworth as:

> ...large and massy; for duration built;
> With pillars crowded, and the roof upheld
> By naked rafters intricately crossed
> Like leafless underboughs in some thick wood,
> All withered by the depth of shade above.

The roof structure is indeed interesting. The floor used to be of beaten earth and once a year would be covered with rushes gathered by the children of the village. Now it is flagged, but the Rushbearing Festival is still celebrated here each August. In the graveyard, near a yew planted by the poet, are the tombs of William Wordsworth, his wife, sister and other members of his family. Near the lych-gate is a small building which was once the school, where Wordsworth taught, and which since 1854 has been the home of Sarah Nelson's Celebrated Grasmere Gingerbread shop.

> The moon was up, the Lake was shining clear
> Among the hoary mountains; from the Shore
> I push'd, and struck the oars and struck again
> In cadence, and my little boat moved on...
> Leaving behind her still on either side
> Small circles glittering idly in the moon,
> Until they melted all into one track
> Of sparkling light.

William Wordsworth, *The Prelude* (1805)

The famous gingerbread shop

GRASSINGTON
North Yorkshire

*T*he Woggins, Jakey, Jacob's Fold and Chamber End Fold – a village with names like these can only be appealing. Indeed, well before the Romans were mining for lead here, Iron Age man had been attracted to the area. In Lea Green, hut circles, Celtic lynchets and dewponds are evidence of the 600-year stay of the Brigantes tribe who were to fight the invading Romans. The euphonious 'folds' that run off the cobbled square and the main street were originally Anglian croft lands, filled in now with grey limestone cottages. Two medieval 'green ways' crossed in Grassington, and in 1381 a weekly market was established by royal charter. Under James I, around 1600, lead ore was extracted up on the moor behind the village and it was these lead mines that were to bring prosperity in the 18th century to this the capital of Upper Wharfedale. Its main square is edged with shops, inns and pleasing houses. In the main street and in the passages off it are harmonious groups of old stone houses and cottages, mainly 17th- and 18th-century, some two- and some three-storey, all coming together to make an exceptionally attractive village. Grassington Hall dates partly from the late 13th century, while Theatre Cottage is a barn converted early in the 19th century to a theatre.

A typical, pretty limestone cottage

HAWORTH
West Yorkshire

3 MILES (4 KM) SOUTH OF KEIGHLEY

Haworth's steep main street, now given over to the visitors who flock in their thousands to this famous village

Haworth is an industrial Pennine village of steep streets and dark stone weavers' cottages. But the industry that is its lifeblood now is not textiles, but the Brontës. For it was in the parsonage here that from 1820 to 1861 the talented Brontë sisters, Charlotte, Emily and Anne lived with their wayward brother Branwell and their father, writing their intensely romantic and powerful novels, including *Jane Eyre* and *Wuthering Heights*. The rapid expansion of the weaving trade in the 18th century had left Haworth's twisted streets cramped with tall terraces of weavers' houses, so grim and grimy and riddled with disease as to horrify Maria Brontë when she arrived with her husband, Reverend Patrick Brontë, and their six children. Two of the children died in childhood, and Maria herself died only a year after moving here. Pilgrims making their devotional way today to the shrine of the Brontë Parsonage Museum toil up the cobbled street that is still the heart of Haworth, above the mills and housing estates in the valley bottom. Resisting if they can the lure of countless cafés and souvenir shops, they reach The Black Bull, one of Branwell's drinking holes, and then the church with its family vault and finally the Parsonage, an 18th-century sandstone building poignantly furnished as it was in the Brontës' day. Beyond are the windswept moors.

The grey churchyard looked greyer, and the lonely churchyard lonelier. I distinguished a moor sheep cropping the short turf on the graves. It was sweet, warm weather – too warm for travelling; but the heat did not hinder me from enjoying the delightful scenery above and below…In winter, nothing more dreary, in summer, nothing more divine, than those glens shut in by hills, and those bluff, bold swells of heath.

Emily Brontë, *Wuthering Heights* (1847)

The tree-shaded banks of the village green, overlooked by the cupola of Fountaine Hospital's elaborate frontage

LINTON-IN-CRAVEN
North Yorkshire

7 MILES (11 KM) NORTH OF SKIPTON

Tall trees, a babbling beck and grassy banks are the setting for the exceptionally grand – for such a modest village – Fountaine Hospital, almshouses founded in 1721. Richard Fountaine, it is said, was in the timber trade, went to London and made his fortune during the Black Death. The almshouses are Classical, very much in the style of Vanbrugh's Castle Howard, which was being constructed at the time not far away. So many echoes are there, in fact, that the suggestion has been made that Fountaine's builder was someone who was also involved in Castle Howard, possibly William Etty (1675–1734). The façade is in fact deceptive, for the building behind is not extensive. Fountaine's name is also commemorated in the tiny pub, standing in trees on the village's irregularly shaped, sloping green. At the foot of the green a ford, stepping stones and three bridges cross the little river, one an ancient clapper bridge, another a 14th-century packhorse bridge and the third a modern road bridge. All around the green are soft limestone houses. Linton Hall is an excellent house that dates basically from the 17th century but has later additions. It has a pretty Dutch-gabled doorway. The church is mainly Norman and delightful, a little away from the centre of its captivating village.

LOWER PEOVER
Cheshire

3 MILES (5 KM) SOUTH OF KNUTSFORD

*L*ower Peover (pronounced 'Peever') is quietly scattered about the fields and woodlands of the Cheshire countryside. At its heart are a few cottages; a pub, Bell's of Peover, named after a former landlord called Bell and once famous for its own ale; two school buildings, the present primary and its little brick, 17th-century predecessor with bell turret at one end, now a private house; and the church. It is the church that makes the village so special, for St Oswald's is one of the oldest timber-framed churches in Europe. In 1269 (and possibly before) there was a chapel here, to which some of the oak beams are believed to date. The stone tower is 16th-century but the striking timber and plasterwork of the nave and chancel are 14th-century. Inside, huge pillars support the superb raftered roof, and rich timberwork is everywhere – on the Jacobean screens, the lectern and pulpit, and on the box pews whose small doors are raised up off the floor to minimise draughts around the ankles. There is an ancient hollowed-out chest; if, as a local lass, you could not lift its hefty lid with one hand, you stood no chance of making a strong and useful farmer's wife.

The village church, one of Cheshire's timber-framed glories

Nailed to a wall in the church is a wooden hand, probably used in medieval days at fairs to indicate that buying and selling were allowed, but also said by locals to represent the miraculous hand of St Oswald. So kind was he to some beggars that he was blessed by St Aidan who declared that the hand that had given so generously would never grow old. And when the rest of his body had long since turned to dust, his hand indeed remained young.

RAMSGILL
North Yorkshire

4 MILES (6.5 KM) NORTH OF PATELEY BRIDGE

*T*he road from Pateley Bridge up Nidderdale runs alongside the beautiful Gouthwaite Reservoir to Ramsgill, a delightful little village at the head of this haven for wildfowl. The road runs across the oval-shaped green around which all Ramsgill's houses stand, their peace and quiet occasionally disturbed by the screech of the peacocks who in the summer months strut about the green or sit up on the church wall. The church recently celebrated the 150th anniversary of its rebuilding in 1842 by the lords of the manor, the Yorke family. The churchyard wall incorporates a small gable from a chapel that was built here by the monks of Byland Abbey. The abbey was given an estate here in 1202 and the monks also built a corn mill and a grange. Edward II stayed at the grange in 1323. After the dissolution, the estate came into the hands of the Yorkes, a family of London merchants. The Yorke Arms, opposite the church, was also rebuilt in the 1840s, and most of the village's attractive grey stone and tiled houses date from that period, though the farmhouse by the church is older. The village does one have one thorn in its side and that is its notorious son, Eugene Aram, a schoolmaster in the mid-18th century who slipped from the straight and narrow and was convicted of murder.

Grey stone cottages bordering the Ramsgill Beck

Contraband

Local smugglers had their heyday in the late 17th and early 18th century. In Ravenscar, at the southern end of the bay, the Raven Hall Hotel still has a 4ft (1.2m) high chamber from which a lantern could be shone out to ships arriving in the bay from the Continent, loaded with goods such as tea, chocolate, playing cards and spirits. The local fishermen would buy the stuff and smuggle it ashore. In 1775 a sergeant and seven soldiers stayed in Robin Hood's Bay trying, to little effect, to wipe out this illegal trade.

A characteristic corner of the village

ROBIN HOOD'S BAY
North Yorkshire

5 MILES (8 KM) SOUTH-EAST OF WHITBY

This one-time fishing village and den of smuggling lies at the northern end of the bay of the same name, above and down a steep ravine, an exhilarating tumble of cottages, shops, chapels and cafés. Below the somewhat prosaic streets of ordinary houses at the top of the hill, the village's main street twists giddyingly down to the sea, at every bend and alleyway and flight of steps turning the kaleidoscope of yellow sandstone, pink pantile, white paint, red and blue flowered window box. Around every corner is another cameo of close-knit gables, doorways and window frames, tiers of stone buildings clinging unbelievably on to rocky ledges. The soft, fossil-rich limestone cliffs are rapidly receding and scores of houses have dissolved into the sea in the last few hundred years. King Street used to be the main way out of the village at the foot of the ravine, until part of the road was swept into the sea in 1780. The Bay Hotel is shored up by a wall to prevent it following its predecessor into the water. A favourite haunt of artists, Bay, or Bay Town as it is known, is also irresistible to the camera-clicking tourist in summer, the trade they bring more or less replacing that of the fisherman.

Houses lead down the steep valley side of Titus Salt's model village

SALTAIRE
West Yorkshire

4 MILES (6.5 KM) NORTH-WEST OF BRADFORD

Saltaire is named after its creator, Sir Titus Salt, the successful Victorian industrialist who in 1850 decided to move his mohair and alpaca factory out from the smoke of Bradford to a site on the River Aire, close to the Yorkshire Dales. Integral to his plan was the building of a village, a complete community for his 3000 workers in which their every need was catered for, a visionary model for the new industrial age. The mill was completed in 1853, a building of massive proportions by Sir William Fairbairn, finished in Italian Renaissance style. By 1872 Salt had built 824 houses. Designed by Lockwood and Mawson, the two- or three-bedroomed sandstone houses were laid out on a grid plan. In addition, Salt provided schools, a hospital, churches and a Congregational chapel, almshouses, baths, a steam laundry and a park – complete, of course, with bandstand. Salt's Mill was pre-eminent among Bradford's textile mills until the 1960s and closed down only in 1985. Today it houses a number of commercial enterprises, as well as the 1853 (David Hockney) Gallery. There is a performance space for theatre and opera in the complex, while the old school is home to Shipley College and the former hospital to a nursing home. As for the mill workers' houses, they are much sought after properties in a village that remains as pleasant as it was in Salt's day.

SLAIDBURN
Lancashire

8 MILES (13 KM) NORTH OF CLITHEROE

The Hark to Bounty
The unusual name of the village inn tells the story of the 19th-century squire and parson named Wigglesworth, who would leave his dog to bark outside the premises. 'Hark', he would say to his drinking companions, 'to Bounty'.

Lying in a fold of the heather and bracken moors where the Croasdale Brook joins the River Hodder, Slaidburn is an old grey stone village that lies on the path of ancient saltways. *Domesday Book* mentions salt-producing centres in Cheshire and south Lancashire and these tracks would have been used by pack ponies carrying salt, essential to meat preservation, from saltpans such as these to outlying farms. Slaidburn was also an administrative centre for the Forest of Bowland, the encircling area of fell and moorland. At the centre of the village stands the Hark to Bounty Inn, a building dating back to the 12th or 13th century whose outside staircase leads up to the courtroom used to settle forest disputes. Petty crimes were tried here as recently as 1937. The houses in this part of the village are all of grey sandstone, set behind cobbled pavements. In Church Street the distinguished school building bears a plaque telling us it was erected and endowed by John Brennand who died in 1717. The church dates back to at least the 13th century. The village green, with the war memorial, is at the lower end of the village, where the road leads out over an old stone bridge across the Hodder and up into the moors.

The shop and the pub, a focal point

The Horse Before the Cart
Some of the earliest evidence
for the use of horse-drawn
wheeled vehicles in Britain
was discovered in Heathery
Burn Cave, up Stanhope Beck.
Quarry workers in the mid-19th
century came across antler
cheek-pieces from horse-bits,
along with the tools and
products of a Late Bronze Age
metal-working family.

STANHOPE
Durham

6 MILES (9.5 KM) WEST OF WOLSINGHAM

*The great tree stump found in
a local quarry*

The massive stump of a fossilised tree stands over the graves in Stanhope churchyard. Believed to be 250 million years old, it came from a nearby quarry. Limestone quarrying, ironstone working and lead mining on the surrounding fells and moors of Upper Weardale brought the village prosperity in the 19th century. Methodism was strong and many of the miners and quarrymen would have attended the chapel. St Thomas's Church, squat and Norman, bounds one side of the small, recently cobbled market square. Its one-time rectory, Stone House, on the east side of the square, was rebuilt in 1824 on the site and in the style of its 1627 predecessor, as a stone in the wall records. On the opposite side is Stanhope Castle, a somewhat forbidding, castellated house built in 1798 on the site of an earlier manor. Close by are some good 18th-century houses, while in the streets radiating out from the square are terraced miners' cottages. From the west end of the village there is a view of Stanhope Hall, a large, tall building with medieval origins. Today Stanhope is a quiet haven for walkers, with footpaths leading in all directions up on to the North Pennine moors or along the banks of the beautiful River Wear.

TROUTBECK
Cumbria

3 MILES (5 KM) NORTH OF WINDERMERE

Townend, an exceptionally well-preserved example of Cumbrian vernacular architecture

Troutbeck stretches for a mile or so along the hillside without any real centre, an inviting succession of enclaves that consist of large, 17th- and 18th-century yeoman or 'statesman' farmhouses, each with its range of buildings and each centred on a well or spring. In the 19th century infill housing was built. The whole village is a delight in vernacular detail, and the observant eye will find much to feast upon. The buildings are of slate, many bare stone, some rendered and painted. A number have the locally typical conical chimneys. Some houses still have their first floor spinning galleries, some their oak-mullioned windows. In the walls are slate drinking troughs for the horses that used the Kirkstone Pass. At the southern end of the village is Townend, a farmhouse built in about 1626 by 'statesman' George Browne and remaining in his family until acquired by the National Trust. Its walls and three massive round chimneys are white-washed, while its splendid barn with its spinning gallery, opposite, is unrendered slate. Its interior is exceptionally well-preserved, with timbering, stone floors and a large farm kitchen. Quite separate from the village is the old school and the church, rebuilt in the 18th century, which has a fine window by Edward Burne-Jones, William Morris and Ford Madox Brown.

Beatrix Potter's 2000 acre (810ha) farm, Troutbeck Park Farm, is one of the most famous sheep farms in the Lake District, with three peaks over 2000ft (608m) high. Her sheep were Herdwicks, tough fell sheep whose wool was traditionally used mainly for rugs. When she died in 1943 she left the farm and its flock to the National Trust.

The castle, 'this worm-eaten hall of ragged stone', is the setting for several scenes in Shakespeare's *Henry IV* plays, for it was here that Henry Percy, Earl of Northumberland, and his son Harry Hotspur hatched their conspiracy against the king.

The view northwards from the castle, over the rooftops and the church

WARKWORTH
Northumberland

7 MILES (11 KM) SOUTH-EAST OF ALNWICK

The view as one crosses the River Coquet, up to the market place and on up the steep main street to the powerful castle ruins at its top, is terrific, in every sense. Warkworth is surrounded on three sides by a loop of the Coquet which is crossed only by a medieval fortified bridge and (for traffic) the adjoining 1960s road bridge. The 14th-century stone bridge and gatehouse is one of a handful of fortified bridges left in the country. Beside it is an imposing 1730s house, and then plain, sturdy, grey stone houses line the street up to the market place and cross. Just back from the square is the church, another spectacular building, almost completely Norman, with the longest nave in Northumberland. In 1174 it witnessed a grim massacre wreaked by Scots on a Border raid. From here is another tremendous view of the castle rearing above the 18th- and 19th-century terraced stone houses that climb on up the main street. The castle was started in the 12th century but its keep, a thing of real beauty in warm stone, with polygonal turrets and a look-out tower, is of early 15th-century date. For 600 years it was the seat of the great Percy family. Still owned by the Duke of Northumberland, it is now in the care of English Heritage.

WYCOLLER
Lancashire

3 MILES (5 KM) EAST OF COLNE

*H*ere is a unique place, a village that was deserted in the 18th century and has now been brought back to life. Hidden away up a dead-end lane in a valley near Trawden Forest, Wycoller was once the home of handloom weavers. Come the Industrial Revolution, and with it power-looms, these people were lured away to the prosperity of Lancashire's rapidly expanding textile towns, never to return. The abandoned cottages began to crumble, the manor house fell into ruins; the pretty beck continued to flow beside its tree-lined banks, but no one crossed its four ancient bridges. Oliver Goldsmith's poem describing the effects of the Revolution on an idyllic village he calls Auburn is said to be based on Wycoller. Charlotte Brontë, living in Haworth some 5 miles (8km) or so across the moors (see page 127), walked here with her sisters and brother and she too was affected by the place, basing the Ferndean Manor of her novel *Jane Eyre* on Wycoller Hall. In 1973 Lancashire County Council designated the village and its surrounding area a country park. The Hall is to be left a ruin, but the half-dozen cottages that were still standing were sold off and life has now been breathed back into their brown-grey stones once more.

Sweet smiling village, loveliest of the lawn,
Thy sports are fled and all thy charms withdrawn;
Amidst thy bowers the tyrant's hand is seen,
And desolation saddens all thy green…
Sunk are thy bowers in shapeless ruin all,
And the long grass o'ertops the mouldering wall;
And trembling, shrinking from the spoiler's hand,
Far, far away, they children leave the land.

Oliver Goldsmith, *The Deserted Village* (1770)

Ancient wooden doorway, Culross

SCOTLAND

O Caledonia! Stern and wild,
Meet nurse for a poetic child!
Land of brown heath and shaggy wood,
Land of my sires! what mortal hand
Can e'er untie the filial band,
That knits me to thy rugged strand!

Sir Walter Scott,
'O Caledonia!'

The railway line between Perth and Inverness was constructed in the 1860s. When it came to bridging the river at Blair Atholl, the engineer, Joseph Mitchell, encountered difficulties with the then Duke who was against railways and agreed to the line passing through his land only on condition the structures blended into the environment. However, the Duchess intervened on Mitchell's behalf and he went on to build a bridge – on his own admission – 'somewhat more ornate than necessary' but an admirable monument to Victorian engineering and design.

Blair Castle, with the big hills of the Forest of Atholl forming a grand, wild background

BLAIR ATHOLL
Perth and Kinross

8 MILES (13 KM) NORTH-WEST OF PITLOCHRY

*T*he Duke of Atholl, owner of Blair Castle, is the only man in Britain to retain a private army, a privilege granted by Queen Victoria. On parade with their pipe band, the Atholl Highlanders, who are all local men, make a magnificently colourful spectacle in front of the white, turreted castle at whose gates the little grey village of Blair Atholl grew up. Many of the villagers are employed on the estates of the castle, the most visited historic house in Scotland. Cumming's Tower dates back to about 1280 but most of the baronial mansion we see today is 18th-century. Set at the foot of Glen Tilt where it meets Glen Garry, it held the key to the central Highlands and saw its share of history over the ages, having associations with Cromwell's men, James V, Mary, Queen of Scots, Montrose and Prince Charlie. In 1746, during the Jacobite Uprising, it underwent what was the last siege laid on British soil. Three bridges cross the River Tilt here. The Old Bridge of Tilt, a centuries-old crossing point used by General Wade for one of his Military Roads, the splendidly ornate, lattice-work Victorian railway bridge and the Bridge of Tilt, which carries the modern road through the village. In the village are a museum, a craft centre and the Old Mill, which still grinds flour.

Highland hills rise behind the streets of Braemar

BRAEMAR
Aberdeenshire

34 MILES (54.5 KM) NORTH OF BLAIRGOWRIE

This is the Highlands at their ravishing best. Heathery hills, a rocky rushing river, the Cairngorm mountains folding away into an ever more blue distance, a dour grey turreted castle, Highland games; the place reeks of history, and there is more than a whiff of royalty too. The village is made up of two former settlements either side of the Clunie, Roman Catholic Auchendryne and Protestant Castleton. In the second half of the 19th century the village was rebuilt with sturdy stone houses, many of which are today the guest-houses that accommodate visitors to the annual Braemar Gathering, which takes place in Memorial Park. The Invercauld Arms Hotel stands on the spot where the 6th Earl of Mar raised the standard to launch the 1715 Rebellion, proclaiming James VIII and III as king, while in one of the cottages in Castleton Terrace, in August 1881, Robert Louis Stevenson wrote the first part of *Treasure Island*. Near the river bridge is Kindrochit Castle. Malcolm Canmore is believed to have built a fortress here, at a meeting of ways across the hills, in the second half of the 11th century but the present castle was built by the Earl of Mar in 1628. Burnt by the Farquharsons 60 years later, it was rebuilt with turrets and crenellations surrounding the original tower-house.

Tradition has it that way back in the 11th century King Malcolm Canmore held martial contests to find the best men to fight with him against the Normans. Certainly Highland gatherings have been held for centuries. The Braemar Games were established in 1832 and Queen Victoria gave them the royal accolade in 1848. The first Saturday in September here is a colourful day of massed pipe bands, dancing, caber-tossing and other athletic events.

The one-oared ferry boat and
the ferryman's house, on the
far side of the Almond

CRAMOND
City of Edinburgh

IN THE NORTH-WESTERN OUTSKIRTS OF EDINBURGH

In 1996 Cramond ferryman, Rab Graham, noticed a stone animal head sticking out of the mud. He tried to remove it, thinking it would look good in his garden. Finding it too big to lift, however, he realized it might be important. Archaeologists were called in and one of the most magnificent pieces of funerary sculpture from Roman Britain was revealed – a crouching lioness, 5ft (1.5m) long, holding a naked man prey in her mouth and paws. She is displayed in the Museum of Scotland in Edinburgh.

Cramond today is a charming place of old white-painted stone cottages that layer steeply down to an ancient quay at the mouth of the River Almond. A ferry boat takes passengers across the narrow estuary to Lord Rosebery's Dalmeny estates. A wooded riverside walk leads past a small boat park to a weir and a ruined mill. A picture postcard image, perhaps, but one that belies its past. On the orders of Emperor Antoninus Pius, around AD142 the Romans built a harbour and fort here, at the eastern end of the Empire's northernmost frontier line. Part of the fort can be seen near the church, a mainly 17th-century building on a site used for many,

many centuries before that. Note its fine carved gravestones. Near by are Cramond Tower, a medieval defensive tower, and Cramond House, home of successive lairds of Cramond. Below it, in the 18th and 19th centuries, the waters of the Almond powered no less than five mills. Originally used for corn and cloth, by 1752 they were manufacturing iron nails, spades, hoops, cart axles and so on. Cockle Mill, closest to the quay where iron was imported and finished products exported, is now a private house. The old workers' cottages have been renovated, while the main forge, Fairafar Mill, is the ruin that stands by the weir – silent testimony to noisier, dirtier days.

CRINAN
Argyll and Bute

6 MILES (9.5 KM) NORTH-WEST OF LOCHGILPHEAD

Crinan is a tiny place at the foot of a wooded rocky promontory beside Loch Crinan. It is also at the western end of the Crinan Canal, and it is this that brings it to life. For yachtsmen it is the gate that opens on to the seas of the Hebrides, and its locks and basin are always busy with the clicking of mainstays and the squeaking and rubbing of fenders. There was little here except a 7th-century church until work started in 1793 on the canal that was to run 9 miles (14.5km) east to Ardrishaig, linking the Sound of Jura with Loch Fyne. This would save ships the slow and hazardous journey around the Mull of Kintyre and speed up deliveries of fish to Glasgow. John Rennie was the chief engineer for the project, which was beset with difficulties from the start. Finances proved a problem, at one point the canal banks collapsed, and what with one thing and another it did not open to traffic until 1809. Even then Thomas Telford had to be called in to make improvements and work continued until 1817. The canal has never been a commercial success but the basin at Crinan today is a popular marina and an attractive setting for the handful of houses and the hotel that has stood here since the 1890s.

A Royal Progress
In 1847 Queen Victoria travelled along the Crinan Canal on her way from Glasgow to Oban, a route which was to be marketed by the ferry company MacBrayne's as the 'Royal Route'. The Royal Route (and, of course, MacBrayne's) feature in Neil Munro's irresistibly comic tales of Para Handy and his 'puffer' boat *Vital Spark*, mostly set in and around Loch Fyne in the first two decades of the 20th century.

The Crinan Hotel, overlooking the locks that open on to the sea

CULROSS
Fife

*I*n the 16th and 17th centuries Culross was one of the largest ports in Scotland with a flourishing trade across the North Sea in local salt and coal. The Industrial Revolution dealt a blow to the economy, the royal burgh of Culross became a backwater, and its narrow, steep, cobbled streets stood still. By careful restoration work, the National Trust for Scotland has created a showpiece here, a treasure trove of 16th-century burgh architecture that looks much as it must have done in its heyday. George Bruce, a coal merchant who played a leading role in Culross's development, in 1597 built himself The Palace. It is a splendid example of a grand town house, built round a courtyard and full of interesting details such as windows half-shuttered in wood (to dodge the window tax), tempera-painted ceilings and a stone-vaulted counting-house. The Town House next door was built in 1626. The Study is an early 17th-century building distinguished by its tower with a little look-out room, and straggling up and down the streets are the so-called 'little houses' of the traders and burghers that give the village its character – white-harled walls beneath grey or red roofs, typical crow-stepped gables, and outside stairs. On the outskirts are the church and ruins of the 13th-century Cistercian abbey.

The Palace, its crow-stepped gables and pantiled roofs characteristic of the local architecture of the period

Wha wad ha' thocht it
Noses wad ha' bocht it?
(Inscription over the old snuffmaker's house, at the top of Tanhouse Brae, dated 1673)

ELIE
Fife

8 MILES (13 KM) EAST OF LEVEN

lie is another of the string of old ports dotted along the coast of Fife that used to trade extensively with cities across the North Sea. Nowadays its safe, sandy beaches are popular in summer with windsurfers and sailors, and many of the attractive old grey stone fishermen's cottages are holiday homes. The bar of the Ship Inn by the harbour has a collection of old pictures of Elie which show how little its layout and buildings have changed over the years. The old granary building on the harbour is being developed to provide a focal point for watersports, and some accommodation. The ground plan of the village is typical of the East Neuk villages, with one main street and narrow wynds leading down to the sea. William Scott of Ardross built the church in 1639 using the T-plan, common in Scotland at the time, that put the pulpit rather than the altar in the centre of the building. The large house in South Street known as The Castle is also of 17th-century date. To the east, towards the East Links golf course, is the lighthouse and Lady's Tower, built as a summerhouse in 1679 for the wife of a local laird, Lady Jane Anstruther. Elie is virtually one and the same place with Earlsferry, whose people, the legend goes, helped Macduff escape from Macbeth.

Lady Jane Anstruther, known as Jenny Falls, used to hold poetry evenings and soirées in her summerhouse by the sea. At the bottom of the tower was her changing room, from which she would emerge to swim naked in the sea, protecting her modesty by sending a bellringer out to warn villagers to keep away.

*The village seen from
Fionnphort harbour*

IONA
Argyll and Bute

5-MINUTE PASSENGER FERRY FROM FIONNPHORT, ISLAND OF MULL

'That man is little to be envied whose…piety would not grow warmer among the ruins of Iona.' So wrote Samuel Johnson in 1775 in *A Journey to the Western Islands of Scotland*. Today, there are some who may find their piety grows warmer, and Iona's special atmosphere is better savoured away from that well-worn sightseers' trail between jetty and abbey, sitting quietly in the wild flowers up on a green hill or walking across the multi-coloured pebbles of a peaceful bay.

The houses of Iona village line the island's eastern shore, their grey gables full face to the ferry that daily brings another influx of pilgrims to this tiny cradle of Christianity. It was here, in AD 563, that St Columba arrived from Ireland to establish a monastery, a base for the missionary journeys that converted the Pictish heathens of the north to his Celtic Christianity. This became a place of holiness, a place of learning, a place of artistic excellence (where work is believed to have begun on *The Book of Kells*), a place of power. Between the 9th century and the Reformation some 48 Scottish kings were buried here, in Reilig Odhrain. Of Columba's monastery little remains, but it was

rebuilt in the 11th century by Queen Margaret and her charming, pink granite Chapel of St Oran is the oldest building on the island. Near it is one of the 350 carved crosses that stood on Iona before the Reformation. Since the turn of the century the Church of Scotland and the Iona Community founded by Lord George MacLeod have carried out extensive restoration work on the abbey. Enjoy the jaunty medieval carvings on some of the piers. The 13th-century nunnery remains a flowery ruin. There are Scottish Episcopal and Roman Catholic retreat houses. Otherwise there is just the village shop, a couple of gift shops, a second-hand bookshop, a café and two hotels.

KILLIN
Stirling

19 MILES (30.5 KM) NORTH OF CALLANDER

Killin's situation is dramatic. At the western end of Loch Tay – a narrow, deep water that snakes beneath the beckoning slopes of Ben Lawers – it sits just where the Falls of Dochart bring the river crashing and swirling and foaming to meet with the River Lochay, a paradise for walkers, fishermen, yachtsmen and skiers. On the village's south-western outskirts whitewashed cottages line the 18th-century Dochart Bridge near the wooded burial island of the Clan MacNab, the most aggressive of several aggressive clans in the area. Killin's white stone church, rebuilt in 1774, originated in the 9th century and its 10th-century font is the only seven-sided one in Scotland. Just to the north of the village are the overgrown ruins of Finlarig Castle, described in Sir Walter Scott's novel *The Fair Maid of Perth*. This was the stronghold of the Campbells and is associated with the notorious Black Duncan of the Cowl. Close by is his 'beheading pit', perhaps the only surviving example. Upper crust wrong-doers were beheaded in it. Lesser mortals were hanged from a nearby tree. In a field near Breadalbane Park a stone is said to mark the burial place of the 3rd-century Celtic warrior hero, Fingal.

The waters of the River Lochay have since the 1950s been harnessed in one of the Highlands hydro-electric power-stations, named after Finlarig Castle. A pipe-line can be seen from the Glen Lochay road, bringing the water from Glen Lyon that turns the turbines. Finlarig is part of the Tummel Bridge hydro-scheme and is controlled from there.

The main street of this summer and winter sports resort, looking towards the green-roofed Episcopal church

The village, set along the ridge of a hill, with the churchyard in the foreground

KILMARTIN
Argyll and Bute

28 MILES (45 KM) SOUTH OF OBAN

John Carswell is remembered now for printing a liturgy in Gaelic in 1567, but for many years after he died, it seems, it was his funeral day that folk recalled. So bad was the weather that his body could not be rowed across from Achnacloich to Ardchattan and thereafter a stormy day was reckoned to be as bad, or nearly as bad, as the day of Carswell's funeral.

Lying just inland from Lochs Crinan and Craignish on the Sound of Jura, the tiny grey village of Kilmartin is the focal point of an area studded with a galaxy of prehistoric sites. The sense of history in this still, quiet glen is all-pervading in its silence. Man has lived here since the dawn of history, probably arriving from across the sea, and over the ages has left a legacy that counts amongst the most inspiring and beautiful in all Scotland.

Just south of the village are the Nether Largie chambered cairns, the most notable of many in a 3-mile (5km), linear pre-Christian cemetery. The Neolithic South Cairn was used for probably over 1000 years for cremated and uncremated bodies. The

Grey recumbent tombs of the dead in desert places,
Standing stones on the vacant wine-red moor,
Hills of sheep, and the homes of the silent vanquished races,
And winds, austere and pure…
Robert Louis Stevenson, '*Blows the wind Today*'

Templewood stone circle

North Cairn is of Bronze Age date and has carved axe-head and cup-and-ring markings. Linear burial sites, found not uncommonly in Wessex, are rare in Scotland, and the carvings of bronze axes found on some of the tombs in this area are otherwise known only at Stonehenge, indicative of close links between Argyll and Wessex. Just west of the South Cairn is the Templewood circle of standing stones. A little further south, rising out of flat land beside the River Add, is the rock on which was built the prehistoric fortress of Dunadd, one of the 6th-century capitals of Dalriada from which the Celtic kingdom of Scotland was created. Near the top are three most poignant carvings in the rock, a man's footprint, a delicate drawing of a boar, and a basin. We can only guess that Scotland's earliest kings washed in the basin and stood in the footprint at their investiture ceremony.

The richness of Celtic art is most beautifully represented in the churchyard at Kilmartin, where there are two famous early Christian crosses. One is finely decorated with plaiting, the other carved with Christ crucified on one side, in Majesty on the other. Also in the graveyard are some splendid, recumbent medieval gravestones, of Malcolms of Poltalloch and Campbells of Duntrune. Richly sculptured and deeply cut, some show knights in armour.

In the village are the ruins of a 16th-century castle, while a little north the remains of Carnasserie Castle overlook the valley. This was also built in the 16th century, by John Carswell, first Protestant Bishop of the Isles – he who printed Knox's liturgy in Gaelic. The ruin still stands five storeys high, with kitchens on the ground floor and a room off the hall on the first floor in which is a finely ornamented fireplace. The views over the glen are beautiful.

NEW LANARK
South Lanarkshire

1 MILE (1.5 KM) SOUTH OF LANARK

Robert Owen was an influential social reformer but some of his ideas failed, notably his 'villages of co-operation', in which each person was to work for the good of the whole, and his Grand National Consolidated Trades Union. He himself recognised that much of his thinking was too advanced. On his deathbed in 1858, he said: 'I gave important truths to the world, and it was only for want of understanding that they were disregarded. I have been ahead of my time.'

Below and opposite: the sandstone factory-workers' homes, built to house eight families each

New Lanark is the most outstanding factory village in Scotland, much of it splendidly restored and revitalised as both a commercial visitor attraction and a living community. In 1784 David Dale and Richard Arkwright chose this narrow, wooded gorge to build new cotton-spinning mills, harnessing the waters of the Falls of Clyde to power their machinery. Initially Dale built four mills and then in 1789 added the 'New Buildings', a four-storeyed block with a bell-tower. He built blocks of tenement housing for the workers, strung along the hillside, and provided them with a church and a workers' institute.

In 1800 the Welshman Robert Owen, Dale's son-in-law, became owner-manager and it is his name that is now most closely associated with New Lanark. Owen introduced radically innovative reforms to the factory working conditions. He reduced working hours and did not allow children to work in the factory until they were ten. In the Institute for the Formation of Character he set up the world's first infant school, and in 1817 built a school for children aged three to ten. He built the Nursery

Buildings to care for the orphan apprentices he found working there. When their contracts expired, the building was used for village housing. He started a scheme for old age pensioners. He improved housing and living conditions: 'I arranged superior stores and shops from which to supply every article of food, clothing etc., which they required...I had the whole of these articles of the best qualities supplied to the people at cost prices...The effect soon became visible in their improved health and superior dress, and the general comfort of their houses.' His philosophy was vindicated by increased output and higher profits, and he persuaded Parliament to incorporate some of his ideas in the Factory Act (1819). New Lanark today is his splendid memorial.

The mills closed in 1968 and by the time the Conservation Trust started work in 1974 the population of the village had fallen to about 80. Today around 200 people live in the restored Georgian buildings. One of the former millworkers' houses has been refurbished to show the living conditions of the 1820s and the 1930s, while Owen's 1813 Village Store houses an exhibition on the original shop, a forerunner of the Co-operative Movement. Robert Owen's life is detailed in his former house. Three mills still stand: No 1 is now a hotel, No 2 houses the Edinburgh Woollen Mill, and there are visitor facilities in No 3. In the main visitor centre there are working textile machines and an audio-visual ride with commentary by an 1820s mill-girl. The Mechanic Workshop and the Dyeworks now house craft workshops.

Corra Linn
Footpaths lead from the village into a nature reserve and along the wooded banks of the river to Corra Linn, the most famous of the Falls of Clyde and an inspiration to poets and painters including Wordsworth, Coleridge and Scott, Turner and Landseer. In 1708 a 'hall of mirrors' was built by the Corra Linn to give visitors the impression of being completely surrounded by water.

Handsome warehouse buildings by the old harbour, reminders of the marble industry's heyday

PORTSOY
Aberdeenshire

5 MILES (8 KM) WEST OF BANFF

The name Portsoy is for most people linked with the green marble quarried just west of the old harbour. Set on a rocky stretch of the Moray Firth coast, the fishing village was declared a Burgh of Barony in 1550 by Mary, Queen of Scots, who gave the charter to the Ogilvies of Boyne. In 1692 Patrick Ogilvie, Lord Boyne, built the old harbour for the development of fishing and for the export of marble to France and elsewhere. To ensure the success of his venture, he also arranged for the importing of marble to be banned. The soft, colourful serpentine was used, chiefly in fireplaces, in great houses all over Britain and the Continent and by the 18th century Portsoy was carrying on a flourishing industry. It is still worked here, on a small scale, and in an old 18th-century warehouse on the harbour front is a shop selling souvenirs and jewellery. Some of the other warehouse and grainstore buildings have been converted for residential use. With the growth of the herring fishing industry, the harbour proved too small and a new one was built by Lord Seafield in 1825. The old stone village is a labyrinth of lanes and wynds, steps up and down, courtyards and crow-stepped gables. The oldest house is Soy House, built in about 1690, and The Star Inn, a one-time smugglers' haunt and now residential, dates from 1727.

ST ABBS
Borders

12 MILES (19 KM) NORTH OF BERWICK

St Abb (Ebba or Aebbe) was the daughter of Edifred, King of Northumbria. Legend has it that she went to sea to escape the attentions of the king of Mercia, was shipwrecked and washed up hereabouts. In gratitude for her safe delivery (from the shipwreck, that is, not the king), she founded a double monastery-nunnery, and governed it as the abbess until she died in AD683. St Cuthbert visited her in 661. The abbey buildings were destroyed, probably by the Vikings, though there are some remains of a later foundation in her name a mile or so inland. The village lived by its fishing (and its smuggling) for centuries; lobster and crab boats still operate from here, but now it is also a holiday village, with one of the few sandy beaches on this spectacular stretch of cliff-bound coast. It clings to the cliffs, some houses looking down from the top, another group of old fishermen's cottages (now holiday homes) lower down, overlooking the little harbour and lifeboat station. Beside the harbour is a picturesque row of ageing wooden net-huts used for storing fishermen's gear. The whole place is brightly coloured, with the orangey-red of pantiled roofs set off by the mix-and-match colours of the painted stone walls of the terraced houses.

Looking down on to the harbour and the lifeboat station

St Abb's Head, just to the north of the village, is a National Nature Reserve, noted particularly for its nesting seabirds, including guillemots, razorbills, kittiwakes, shags, fulmars and eiders. The walk out there from the village along the cliffs, with the North Sea pounding below, is a spectacular one. Alternatively, there are trips from the harbour to the point.

Farewell to the mountains high
cover'd with snow;
Farewell to the Straths and
green vallies below:
Farewell to the forests and
wild-hanging woods;
Farewell to the torrents and
loud-pouring floods.

My heart's in the Highlands,
my heart is not here;
My heart's in the Highlands a
chasing the deer;
Chasing the wild deer, and
following the roe;
My heart's in the Highlands,
wherever I go…

Robert Burns, 'My Heart's in
the Highlands' (1790)

The village shelters beneath
sandstone crags, alongside
the loch's shingly shore

SHIELDAIG
Highland

7 MILES (11 KM) WEST OF TORRIDON

'On a beautiful day,' wrote the venerable A Wainwright, 'Shieldaig is a reminder of heaven'. A single row of low, harled and whitewashed houses lines the curving, pebbly shore of Loch Shieldaig, an inlet of Loch Torridon, facing across to the green bump of Shieldaig Island and backed by craggy grey rocks and majestic purple mountains. The Vikings, too, were attracted to the place, calling it *Sild-vik*, Herring Bay. In about 1800, during the Napoleonic Wars, an Admiralty scheme to encourage the growth of fishing communities in the Highlands – and thereby boost numbers of recruitable seamen – gave grants for boat-building, guaranteed fish prices and exempted the people from the salt tax. The fishermen and crofters of the newly created village of Shieldaig prospered for a while, but with the end of the wars came the end of the Government scheme, and left to its own devices the community declined. Today some of the houses are holiday homes for those who come to explore the glorious country around this quiet, unassuming little place. In the bay is a National Trust for Scotland reserve, pine-clad Shieldaig Island. Beyond the waters of the loch rise Torridon's mighty peaks, to the south-east is Beinn Damh. The coastal road west to Applecross offers insatiable views across to Raasay and Skye.

In 1787 William Cruickshank detected the element strontium in the mineral strontianite that was found in the lead mines here and in 1808 Sir Humphry Davy (of the miners' safety lamp) isolated the yellow metal. It is used in the manufacture of fireworks and red signal flares. The isotope strontium-90, which is formed by nuclear explosions, is considered the most hazardous constituent in radio-active fall-out.

STRONTIAN
Highland

20 MILES (32 KM) SOUTH-WEST OF FORT WILLIAM

A new heart for an old Highland village

Strontian gives its name to the metallic element strontium. The village lies at the foot of Strontian Glen and it was in the lead mines in the upper glen that, in 1764, the mineral named strontianite, the original source of strontium, was first found. This brought the village some prosperity, but its heyday ended with the closure of the mines in 1904. However, towards the end of the 1960s the Department of Agriculture and Fisheries for Scotland initiated a scheme to revitalise small villages such as Strontian and a programme of new building got under way. The village still has some old houses and hotels, but it has a modern nucleus in a complex of buildings that includes a shop, sheltered housing for the elderly, a surgery, the primary school and a football park. A number of new houses were also built, and now more new houses, many of them holiday homes, are going up. All are shown off to their best advantage by the village's setting at the mouth of a wooded glen. The River Strontian runs through the village and out on to the red-sand shores of Loch Sunart. In the background looms Ben Resipol. The old mines were recently reopened for a few years to extract barytes needed by the oil industry, but now the only employment is in tourism.

The monument to Nelson, erected immediately after the battle of Trafalgar, 37 years before the column in London's Trafalgar Square

TAYNUILT
Argyll and Bute

9 MILES (14.5 KM) EAST OF OBAN

On a grassy hillock overlooking the village, near the parish church, is a 12ft (3.5m) high granite pillar that is the earliest monument to Nelson in Britain. Something of a surprise in a West Highland village, particularly as, at the start of the 19th century, there was more sympathy in these parts for the Auld Alliance with France than for the 1707 Act of Union with England. The explanation lies in the charcoal blast-furnace works on the shore of Loch Etive, fully restored to working order and open to the public. Banned from tree-felling in England, iron-smelters moved their furnaces to Scotland and in 1753 a company in Cumbria established a furnace at Taynuilt, which, being heavily forested in oak and beech, was well able to supply the necessary charcoal. Iron ore was brought up from Ulverston to Kelly's Pier and some 600 men, many from Lancashire, were employed in the manufacture of pig iron. Most of the village's granite houses date from this period. It was these furnacemen who in 1805 erected the monument to Nelson. In 1874 the 'bloomery' closed, put out of business by the introduction of blast furnaces, and the village became the quiet place it is today, a haunt of fishermen, nature-lovers and walkers who explore the beautiful countryside around about. Taynuilt is a stop on the magnificently scenic Glasgow-to-Oban line.

WANLOCKHEAD
Dumfries and Galloway

6 MILES (9.5 KM) NORTH-EAST OF SANQUHAR

A Lowlands village, this, but one that has the distinction of being the highest in all of Scotland. It is 1531ft (465m) above sea level, set in the rounded green and brown Lowther Hills. In the 17th century these hills were the hiding-place of the Presbyterian Covenanters, persecuted so mercilessly in the cause of religious freedom. Now sheep graze free-range, even in the village itself. Many of the village's whitewashed stone houses are around the head of Wanlock Water. Most of the single-storey cottages were built between the mid-18th and the mid-19th centuries, the homes of miners, for between 1680 and 1934 the villagers lived by lead mining – though gold and silver too have been mined in the area since Roman times. The story of the local mines is told in the Museum of Scottish Lead Mining, where visitors can go on a tour of an 18th-century lead mine, a smelt mill and miners' cottages furnished in the styles of 1740 and 1890. Also here is the Miners' Reading Society Library, founded in 1756 and the second oldest subscription library in Britain. It is not all past history, however, for in 1992 the world gold-panning championships were held here, with the Duke of Buccleugh (whose mid-19th century ancestors did much to improve miners' housing) waiving his mineral rights for the duration.

An 'adit' entrance to a lead mine, seen at the museum

The story of the Lowlands Covenanters and the extremes to which their religious enthusiasm took them is inseparably linked with Sir Walter Scott's *Old Mortality* (1816). The novel is based on anecdotes told by 'Old Mortality', a supporter of their cause who goes around cleaning up their tombs, and in particular tells the love story of the courageous young Covenanter, Morton, and Edith, grand-daughter of his Royalist opponent.

INDEX